CAMPAIGN 328

IMJIN RIVER 1951

Last Stand of the 'Glorious Glosters'

BRIAN DROHAN

ILLUSTRATED BY STEVE NOON

Series Editor Marcus Cowper

OSPREY
Bloomsbury Publishing Plc
PO Box 883, Oxford, OX1 9PL, UK
1385 Broadway, 5th Floor, New York, NY 10018, USA
E-mail: info@ospreypublishing.com
www.ospreypublishing.com

OSPREY is a trademark of Osprey Publishing Ltd

First published in Great Britain in 2018

A catalogue record for this book is available from the British Library.

ISBN: PB 9781472826923; eBook 9781472826916; ePDF 9781472826909; XML 9781472826930

18 19 20 21 22 10 9 8 7 6 5 4 3 2 1

Maps by Bounford.com
3D BEVs by The Black Spot
Index by Nick Hayhurst
Typeset by PDQ Digital Media Solutions, Bungay, UK
Printed in China through World Print Ltd.

DEDICATION

For my grandparents, Tom Rowan and Choe Kyung-suk, who made Korea their home for over 20 years.

ARTIST'S NOTE

Readers may care to note that the original paintings from which the colour plates in this book were prepared are available for private sale. All reproduction copyright whatsoever is retained by the publishers. All enquiries should be addressed to:

www.steve-noon.co.uk

The publishers regret that they can enter into no correspondence upon this matter.

Osprey Publishing supports the Woodland Trust, the UK's leading woodland conservation charity. Between 2014 and 2018 our donations are being spent on their Centenary Woods project in the UK.

To find out more about our authors and books, visit **www.ospreypublishing.com**. Here you will find extracts, author interviews, details of forthcoming events and the option to sign up for our newsletter.

IMPERIAL WAR MUSEUMS COLLECTIONS

Many of the photos in this book come from the huge collections of IWM (Imperial War Museums) which cover all aspects of conflict involving Britain and the Commonwealth since the start of the twentieth century. These rich resources are available online to search, browse and buy at www.iwm.org.uk/collections. In addition to Collections Online, you can visit the Visitor Rooms where you can explore over 8 million photographs, thousands of hours of moving images, the largest sound archive of its kind in the world, thousands of diaries and letters written by people in wartime, and a huge reference library. To make an appointment, call (020) 7416 5320, or e-mail mail@iwm.org.uk
Imperial War Museums www.iwm.org.uk

Key to military symbols

CONTENTS

Korea, June 1950

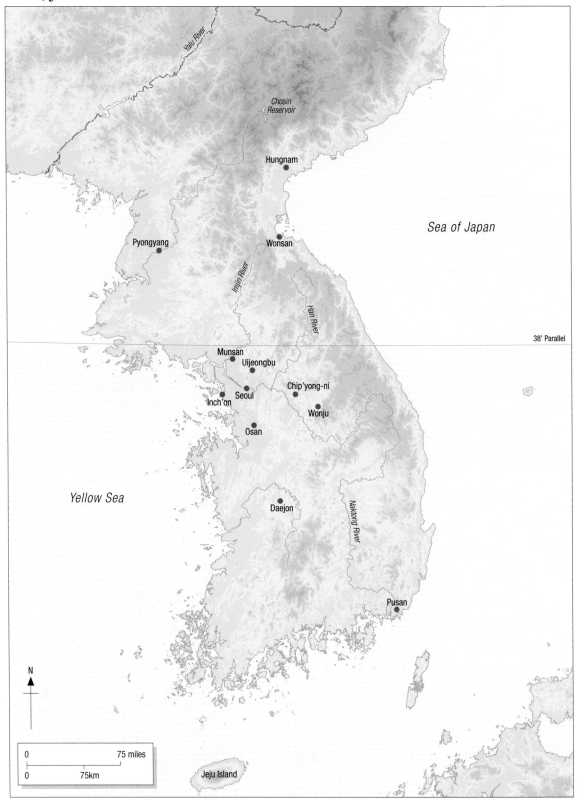

Yalu River

Chosin Reservoir

Hungnam

Sea of Japan

Pyongyang

Wonsan

Imjin River

Han River

38' Parallel

Munsan
Uijeongbu
Chip'yong-ni
Seoul
Inch'on
Wonju
Osan

Yellow Sea

Daejon

Naktong River

Pusan

N

0 ____ 75 miles
0 ____ 75km

Jeju Island

ORIGINS OF THE CAMPAIGN

In April 1951, with the outcome of the Korean War very much in doubt, the destruction of 1st Battalion, the Gloucestershire Regiment on a hill south of the Imjin River was lauded as a gallant last stand – yet another heroic sacrifice by plucky British soldiers in a distant land. Nicknamed the 'glorious Glosters', the men were memorialized in newspapers and radio broadcasts throughout the United Kingdom. One story published in the *Illustrated News* evoked the First World War poet Rupert Brooke's poem 'The Soldier', describing the site of the Glosters' stand as 'a corner of Korea "that is for ever England" '. Although the Glosters gained much of the fame, the battle of the Imjin River was defined by more than their last stand – the entire British 29th Infantry Brigade was engaged in a desperate, four-day fight to defend a key point in the line during a critical phase of what is today often considered a forgotten war.

OUTBREAK OF THE KOREAN WAR

The empire of Japan annexed Korea in 1910, although it had intervened in Korean affairs for decades previously. With the end of World War II, Japan relinquished its claim to Korea. The victorious allies had agreed to place Korea under an international trusteeship in preparation for full independence. As part of this agreement, the two superpowers of the Soviet Union and United States each occupied part of Korea – the Soviets controlled the area north of the 38th Parallel; the US took charge of the territory south of the 38th Parallel. However, ideological rivalry between the communist Soviets and the democratic, capitalist US grew rapidly throughout the late 1940s. Competition between Soviet-backed communist regimes and US-supported anti-communists led to conflict and political tension: the 1946 Iran Crisis, 1946–49 Greek Civil War, 1945–49 Chinese Civil War, and the 1948–49 Berlin Blockade (to which the Western allies responded with the Berlin Airlift) were all part of the beginning of a global Cold War.

These emerging Cold War tensions also shaped Korean politics. By 1947, the Soviets and Americans realized that they could not agree on a common path towards Korean

British soldiers earned two medals for service in Korea. The Korea Medal (*left*) was a campaign medal awarded to soldiers from Commonwealth states. Troops from United Nations member states also received the United Nations Service Medal (*right*). (IWM, OMD 4046)

American troops march towards the Naktong River during operations around the Pusan Perimeter in August 1950. Heading in the opposite direction, Korean refugees flee from the North Korean onslaught. (Bettmann/ Getty Images)

independence. Furthermore, Korean domestic politics were also fractured, as communists under Kim Il-sung dominated North Korea and right-wing nationalists under Syngman Rhee came to power in South Korea. In 1948, South Korea held elections under United Nations (UN) supervision. Syngman Rhee won the election and became the first President of the Republic of Korea (ROK), as South Korea was officially named. The Soviets responded by installing Kim Il-sung as the Premier of the Democratic People's Republic of Korea (DPRK), the formal title of North Korea.

Far from being mere pawns of the superpowers, Rhee and Kim each pursued their own agendas. Rhee's government in the ROK claimed to represent all of Korea, not just the south, which directly challenged the DPRK's legitimacy.

US Marines scale the seawall at Red Beach during the September 1950 Inch'on landings. (Getty, Interim Archives)

Kim, meanwhile, sought to subvert the ROK government through an armed insurgency. This rebellion reached its height from October 1948 to January 1949. South Korean forces loyal to Rhee successfully suppressed the insurgency, but Kim redoubled his efforts in March 1950 by sending North Korean guerrillas to reinvigorate the rebellion. When this too failed, Kim decided on a full-scale invasion of the south.

After securing support from mainland China – the communist People's Republic of China under Mao Zedong – and the Soviet Union, Kim ordered the North Korean People's Army to launch a massive offensive across the 38th Parallel. On 25 June 1950, the invasion began. It took the poorly trained and under-resourced ROK Army completely by surprise. With nearly 230,000 soldiers, 120 Soviet-supplied T-34/85 tanks and 180 Soviet-made aircraft at its disposal, the North Korean army captured the South Korean capital, Seoul, after only three days. As North Korean troops surged towards Seoul, the UN Security Council met in New York. The Soviet Union, which could veto any resolution due to its status as a permanent member of the Council, had been boycotting Security Council proceedings, so the Soviet delegation was not present to challenge two UN resolutions that condemned the North Korean attack, urged an end to hostilities and encouraged UN member states to assist South Korea. On 7 July, the UN Security Council passed a third resolution calling for the establishment of a United Nations Command, under American leadership, to defend South Korea. Fifteen states sent fighting contingents in support of this call.

The CPVA 119th Division crossing the Yalu in October 1950. The CPVA was a battle-tested force that had defeated the Nationalist Chinese and unified mainland China under communist rule. (Sovfoto/Getty Images)

In the days after the invasion, the US rushed troops from Japan to South Korea to bolster the ROK Army. These units had been performing occupation duties, but were not ready for the North Korean onslaught. On 5 July, a reinforced battalion from the US 24th Infantry Division, named Task Force Smith after its commanding officer, was overrun by North Korean armoured forces near the town of Osan. The rest of the 24th Division staged a delaying act further south at Daejon, but it too was defeated. Finally, in late August during a series of battles around Daegu and along the Naktong River, ROK and US forces led by Lt. Gen. Walton Walker (who commanded Eighth US Army, the ground force headquarters in Korea) and supported by US airstrikes, stopped the North Korean advance. The North Koreans continued assaulting US and ROK forces around the defensive lines that had become known as the Pusan Perimeter, which protected the vital port of Pusan, but North Korean strength was diminishing as UN Command forces were being reinforced with heavy weapons and manpower. British troops from the 27th Commonwealth Brigade were the first non-US contingent to arrive.

UN RESURGENCE AND CHINESE INTERVENTION

Taking advantage of the growing strength of UN forces, General of the Army Douglas MacArthur, the US officer in overall command of the war effort, planned a counteroffensive. On 15 September, MacArthur ordered the newly formed X Corps, comprising the US 7th Infantry and 1st Marine Divisions, to conduct an amphibious assault at Inch'on, a port city on Korea's west coast approximately 24km (15 miles) from Seoul. The Inch'on landing surprised the North Korean leadership and, combined with a simultaneous attempt by UN forces to break out of the Pusan Perimeter, routed what remained of the North Korean army. By landing at Inch'on, MacArthur outflanked the North Koreans, who had remained committed to breaking through the Pusan defences. With their rear now threatened and facing sustained air attacks, the North Korean army retreated rapidly to Seoul in an effort to stage a last-ditch defence of the city. Pressed from the west by X Corps and from the south by a newly resurgent Eighth Army, the North Koreans could not hold on. UN forces captured Seoul on 27 September.

The UN victory in the south was decisive. The North Korean army was shattered. MacArthur prepared to send UN forces north of the 38th Parallel to unify the Korean peninsula. On 1 October, ROK troops crossed the 38th Parallel, followed several days later by other UN forces. Eighth Army advanced up the west coast, capturing Pyongyang on 19 October, while ROK forces and X Corps moved north along the east coast. On 21 November, ROK troops reached the Yalu River, which marked the border between Korea and China.

The communist powers, however, were shocked. China and the Soviet Union did not want to see the unification of Korea by anti-communist forces because such a victory would allow the United States to position troops along Korea's northern borders with China and the Soviet Union. In North Korea, Kim Il-sung was desperate for help. After the success of the Inch'on landings became apparent, Soviet, North Korean and Chinese leaders discussed the possibility of military intervention. However, the Soviets did not want to risk a direct military confrontation with the US. Mao Zedong saw the UN forces' success as enough of a threat that he felt compelled to intervene in the conflict. The Soviets promised to provide military equipment and air support. On 2 October, Mao informed the Soviet leader Josef Stalin of his intention to despatch a force of 300,000 'volunteers' to support North Korea.

Chinese intervention dramatically changed the course of the war. The initial Chinese assault occurred on 1 November, but was limited to spoiling attacks designed to slow the UN advance. The main offensive came on 25 November. Employing night attacks and infiltration tactics to encircle UN forces, the Chinese drove UN troops south in a rout. The US 2nd Division was cut off and waged a fighting retreat to escape encirclement, suffering 5,000 casualties in the process. To the east, at the Chosin Reservoir, the US 1st Marine Division was also surrounded. Facing bitterly cold, sub-zero temperatures and heavy snows, the Marines fought their way to safety while enduring a 17-day march to re-join the rest of X Corps. Approximately 4,400 Marines were killed, wounded or captured during the withdrawal. Under intense pressure from the Chinese People's Volunteer

During the battle of the Chosin Reservoir, US Marines endured below-freezing temperatures as they withdrew, largely on foot, to escape encirclement by three Chinese divisions. Throughout the ordeal, the Marines remained organized and disciplined. (Historical/ Getty Images)

Army (CPVA), UN forces retreated south of the 38th Parallel. In a matter of weeks, UN troops had seen their chance for a swift victory turn into a catastrophic retreat.

To make matters worse, Lt. Gen. Walker died in a jeep accident on 23 December. He was replaced by Lt. Gen. Matthew Ridgway. A World War II veteran, Ridgway had commanded the 82nd Airborne Division and, later, the XVIII Airborne Corps in north-west Europe. He had a reputation as being tough, determined and an inspirational leader. Immediately upon taking command, he set about instilling confidence in what was then a demoralized organization. Ridgway regularly visited the front line and demanded that his division and corps commanders lead by example. He also changed the way that UN forces operated by emphasizing the importance of attrition in wearing down the Chinese. Ridgway's approach stressed the importance of killing large numbers of the enemy rather than capturing ground. He issued standing orders to minimize UN casualties while maximizing enemy casualties. In doing so, Ridgway relied on the UN forces' superior firepower in the form of artillery, tanks and airpower. He believed that this attritional approach would exhaust the Chinese over time, thereby forcing them to negotiate a peace settlement. Ridgway intended to conduct a planned, orderly retreat south of the Han River, which would leave the Chinese vulnerable by overextending their supply lines. Once the Chinese were overextended, Ridgway planned to counter-attack.

RIDGWAY'S OFFENSIVES

As Ridgway circulated the battlefield to reinvigorate his force, the Chinese advance continued. On 7 January 1951, the Chinese and accompanying North Korean forces captured Seoul. However, as the Chinese pushed south of Seoul, their advance began to slow. Resupplying Chinese troops became increasingly difficult due to the sub-zero temperatures and long

Chinese capture US troops near Wonsan, North Korea, in January 1951. The CPVA captured thousands of UN troops during the often-chaotic withdrawal from North Korea. (PhotoQuest/Getty Images)

distances involved. At this point, Ridgway seized the opportunity to launch his counteroffensive. On 25 January, he initiated Operation *Thunderbolt*, in which UN forces conducted a slow, methodical advance northwards supported by heavy artillery fire and air support. By 9 February, Eighth Army had reached the Han River. A quick Chinese offensive on 11 February made some initial gains, but was halted at Wonju and Chip'yong-ni after suffering severe casualties.

Throughout February and March 1951, Ridgway launched a series of limited offensives, beginning with Operation *Killer* on 20 February, that were designed to maximize enemy casualties. No attack was to be launched in unfavourable circumstances. Instead, these assaults would be well coordinated and supported by artillery and airstrikes. These gradual, systematic offensives slowly pushed the Chinese back, with UN forces recapturing Seoul on 14 March. After consulting with the US Joint Chiefs of Staff, Ridgway received permission to cross the 38th Parallel in order to occupy more defensible terrain several miles to the north.

Ridgway planned his next offensive, Operation *Rugged*, as another limited-objective offensive intended to seize a series of positions that UN planners named Line Kansas. Line Kansas ran along the Imjin River in the west, towards the Hwacheon Reservoir, and east

A Korean woman and two children survive in a makeshift shelter. The fighting in and around Seoul during 1950 and 1951 devastated the city and destroyed many civilians' livelihoods. (Bert Hardy/ Picture Post/Hulton Archive/ Getty Images)

to Yangyang on the coast. The centre part of the line, from the Imjin River to the Hwacheon Reservoir, ran approximately 3–10km (2–6 miles) north of the 38th Parallel. East of the Hwacheon Reservoir, the line lay about 16km (10 miles) north of the 38th Parallel. In addition to providing good defensive terrain along river banks and hilltops, Line Kansas could also serve as a staging area for future attacks northwards into the 'Iron Triangle', an area under North Korean control that was named after the numerous railways and roads that criss-crossed the region. Line Kansas would position UN forces approximately 24–32km (15–20 miles) south of the Iron Triangle. Operation *Rugged* began on 2 April.

A second, smaller offensive, Operation *Dauntless*, began after the forces involved in Operation *Rugged* occupied Line Kansas. Involving I Corps and IX Corps, the idea behind Operation *Dauntless* was to advance to Line Utah and Line Wyoming, which ran east-to-west along high ground that dominated the southernmost part of the Iron Triangle. By seizing Lines Utah and Wyoming, UN forces could threaten the Iron Triangle without

Lieutenant-General Matthew B. Ridgway replaced Walton Walker as Eighth Army commander. In addition to his no-nonsense leadership style, he was known for his distinctive 'look' – he always wore a hand grenade on his web gear and pinned airborne wings on his hat. (Bettmann/Getty Images)

capturing it. At this point, Ridgway did not want his forces drawn into a full-fledged assault on the Iron Triangle because intelligence reports suggested that the Chinese and North Koreans were preparing an offensive of their own, although Ridgway did not yet know the timing, strength or location of the upcoming enemy assault. By 22 April, when the Chinese offensive began, UN forces had occupied Line Kansas and much (but not all) of Line Utah, but were 8–16km (5–10 miles) south of Line Wyoming.

As UN troops moved slowly but inexorably forwards during Ridgway's methodical offensives, UN high command experienced a dramatic shake-up. Just as the UN landing at Inch'on shocked the communist powers into further escalation of the war, the Chinese intervention stimulated debate in the United States about whether to strike China, either with conventional forces or atomic weapons. President Truman agreed with other leaders such as Prime Minister Clement Atlee of Britain that the war should remain limited to the Korean peninsula. Conversely, MacArthur sought to widen the war. He advocated blockading China, striking its air and naval facilities and launching attacks against mainland China, using Nationalist Chinese troops on Taiwan. MacArthur openly discussed his disagreement with congressmen in the United States and made public statements expressing his desire to widen the war. Truman refused to allow such insubordination and, on 11 April 1951, he relieved MacArthur of command. Truman then chose to promote Ridgway to the rank of general and appointed him commander of all UN forces in Korea. As the MacArthur controversy brewed, Operations *Rugged* and *Dauntless* were meeting with success and the British 29th Brigade was settling into defensive positions along the Imjin River, part of Line Kansas.

CHRONOLOGY

1950

25 June	The Democratic People's Republic of Korea (DPRK, or North Korea) invades the Republic of Korea (ROK, or South Korea), initiating the Korean War.
28 June	North Korean troops capture Seoul.
5 July	Task Force Smith, from the US 24th Infantry Division, is defeated in the United States Army's first ground combat engagement with North Korean forces.
13 July	Eighth US Army headquarters established for the defence of Korea.
14 July	ROK armed forces placed under the United Nations Command.
8–18 August	UN forces stop the North Korean offensive at the Second Battle of the Naktong, outside Pusan.
15 September	UN forces conduct an amphibious landing at Inch'on.
27 September	UN troops liberate Seoul.
30 September	ROK forces move north of the 38th Parallel.
2 October	Mao Zedong informs Soviet leader Josef Stalin of his intention to intervene in the war.
19 October	Eighth Army captures Pyongyang, the North Korean capital.
25 November	After several small-scale skirmishes between UN and Chinese forces, the main Chinese offensive begins.
27 November –13 December	Battle of the Chosin Reservoir.

1951

7 January	Chinese and North Korean forces capture Seoul for the second time.
25 January –20 February	Eighth Army launches Operation *Thunderbolt*, the first of a series of limited-objective UN counteroffensives.
13-18 February	UN troops defeat a Chinese counter-attack.
20 February	Operation *Killer* begins.
7 March	Operation *Ripper* begins.
14–15 March	ROK 1st Division and US 3rd Division recapture Seoul.
2 April	Operation *Rugged* begins.

11 April	Operation *Dauntless* begins in Korea as US President Truman relieves General of the Army Douglas MacArthur for insubordination. General Ridgway replaces MacArthur as supreme commander.
22 April	The Chinese Spring Offensive begins.
22–25 April	Battle of the Imjin River.
22–25 April	Battle of Kap'yong.
25 April	I Corps withdraws to Line Delta.
26 April	Under continued Chinese pressure, I Corps withdraws to positions 3–8km (2–5 miles) south of Line Delta.
28 April	As UN forces continue to retreat, I Corps occupies Line Golden, north of Seoul, with orders to hold at all costs.
28–30 April	The Chinese offensive stalls, forcing Chinese commanders to halt and reorganize.
1–14 May	UN forces counter-attack, making limited gains.
16 May	Having regrouped, the Chinese offensive resumes with assaults in the middle of the peninsula, but UN forces quickly defeat these attacks and the offensive runs out of momentum.
20 May	UN counteroffensive drives the Chinese and North Korean armies north of the 38th Parallel across most of the front line.
15 June–1 July	UN forces fight their way north along a front tracing Line Kansas in the west and east, with a bulge to the north along Line Wyoming in the centre of the peninsula. UN forces begin fortifying this line in preparation for a long war of attrition. With some variations, this line approximates the Demilitarized Zone (DMZ) that separates North and South Korea to this day.
10 July	Armistice negotiations begin at the city of Kaesong; after two years of negotiations, the armistice was finally signed on 27 July 1953.

OPPOSING COMMANDERS

CHINESE COMMANDERS

At the time, the Chinese People's Liberation Army (PLA) did not use traditional military ranks. Instead, and in tune with the strict egalitarianism of its communist ideology, the PLA employed a system of 'positional titles' designed to prevent elitism. Leaders received titles based on the position they held. This procedure was continued into the Chinese People's Volunteer Army (CPVA) in Korea, which was commanded by the short-tempered, stubborn, but highly experienced and canny 51-year-old, **Peng Dehuai**.

An experienced and determined commander, Peng Dehuai led Chinese forces during the Spring 1951 Offensive. (Sovfoto/UIG via Getty Images)

Born into a poor peasant family, Peng joined a Chinese warlord's army in Hunan Province, then later joined the Nationalist Chinese army under Chiang Kai-Shek, where he became a brigade commander. In 1928, he switched sides to fight for Mao Zedong's Chinese Communist Party. After the Japanese invasion of Manchuria in 1937, Peng fought against the Japanese until the end of World War II. He was then named commander of communist forces in north-west China, where he led several successful offensives against the Nationalists during the Chinese Civil War of 1945–49. In 1949, he was named vice-chairman of the Central Military Committee. During initial discussions concerning whether to commit Chinese forces to the Korean War, Peng was one of very few senior military officers to advocate in favour of intervention.

Furthermore, Peng had a close relationship with Mao. He had fought with Mao during the 1934–35 Long March, which was the most trying time for Mao as a communist guerrilla leader during the Chinese Civil War. At that time, Mao's forces had been badly beaten by the Nationalists. To escape certain destruction, Mao initiated a year-long, 8,000-km (5,000-mile) retreat from southern China, through the western interior, and into the north of the country, where the communists regrouped. Many of Mao's closest confidants were people who had remained committed to him during the dark days of the Long March. Although Mao remained the supreme decision-maker on issues of policy and strategy, he trusted Peng's judgement.

For the opening phase of the Spring Offensive, Peng tasked the XIX Army Group with attacking ROK 1st Division and the British 29th Brigade along the Imjin River. The XIX Army Group commander, 41-year-old **Yang Dezhi**, had served with Peng for many years and was known for his unquestioning obedience to orders. Yang had joined the Chinese Red Army as a private in 1928. Like Peng, Yang had participated in the Long March and later rose to command a brigade during the war with Japan. During the Chinese Civil War, he commanded at the Army Group level on two occasions.

The XIX Army Group's 63rd Army was assigned the mission of assaulting the British 29th Brigade. 63rd Army's commander, **Fu Chongbi**, was yet another Long March veteran and had spent most of his military service as a political commissar. Commanding the 187th Division of 63rd Army – the spearhead of the assault – was 30-year-old **Xu Xin**. Xu led a battalion against the Japanese and commanded a regiment during the Chinese Civil War. After the war, he served as the 187th Division's chief of staff before being appointed as its commander. Although he was exceptionally young for a division commander, Xu, like all other Chinese senior leaders, had many years of experience in both guerrilla and conventional warfare.

Gen. James A. Van Fleet was named Eighth Army commanding general less than two weeks before the Chinese offensive along the Imjin River. (Michael Rougier/ The LIFE Picture Collection/ Getty Images)

UN COMMANDERS

Although soldiers from 15 UN states fought in Korea, UN senior leaders were predominantly American. With Gen. Ridgway having been promoted to overall commander, Eighth Army received a new leader – **Lt. Gen. James A. Van Fleet**. Van Fleet led a battalion during World War I and commanded at the regimental, divisional and corps levels during World War II. Prior to arriving in Korea, Van Fleet had led the United States' advisory mission to Greece during the Greek Civil War of 1946–49. He commanded Second US Army, based in Maryland, from 1950 until he was called to Korea.

I Corps, which would face the main effort of the Chinese offensive, was commanded by the experienced **Lt. Gen. Frank Milburn**, who had commanded at corps level in north-western Europe during World War II. The US 3rd Infantry Division, to which the British 29th Brigade was attached, was led by **Maj. Gen. Robert Soule**. Soule led a glider infantry regiment in the Pacific theatre during World War II and was a decorated combat leader, having won the Distinguished Service Cross and Silver Star Medal for valour in action.

British commanders were also highly experienced. All of 29th Brigade's battalion commanders and the brigade commander had led forces of comparable size during World War II. The brigade commander, **Brig. Tom**

Brigadier Tom Brodie was a former Chindit Brigade commander during the Second World War who was highly respected by his men. (Cheshire Military Museum)

Brodie, led a Chindit Brigade in Burma during the war. Unsurprisingly, Brodie was accomplished at jungle warfare and long-range patrolling. He frequently circulated among his troops, often with a swagger stick in hand. His cheerful confidence inspired the men of the brigade.

The British battalion commanders were likewise proven combat leaders who were well respected by their subordinates. **Lieutenant-Colonel Kingsley Foster** grew up in an army family. Foster commanded 1st Battalion, the Royal Northumberland Fusiliers and was seen by his troops as a kindly father figure – a perception that drove younger officers to try to impress him. **Lieutenant-Colonel James 'Fred' Carne** commanded 1st Battalion, the Gloucestershire Regiment. His background was in the colonies, where he led a battalion of the King's African Rifles against the Japanese during World War II. He was notoriously taciturn and had a habit of always carrying a pipe. Some considered him old-fashioned and unimaginative, but he led by example and was calm under pressure. This coolness under fire gave rise to his nickname: 'Cool Carne'. The commander of 1st Battalion, the Royal Ulster Rifles was on leave during the Imjin battle. Instead, the Rifles were led by their second-in-command, **Maj. Gerald Rickord**. Rickord began his career patrolling the mountains of the north-west frontier in India before leading a glider

Lieutenant-Colonel Carne shown at the end of the war, with his ubiquitous pipe in hand. (Soldiers of Gloucestershire Museum)

infantry battalion during World War II. Despite his relaxed personality, he was known for his toughness, professional competence and willingness to take the initiative.

Two other manoeuvre forces that played a key role in the battle were C Squadron, 8th King's Royal Irish Hussars, and the Belgian infantry battalion. C Squadron was led by **Maj. Henry Huth**, who was quick-witted and known for his personal courage. He had fought against the German Afrika Korps during World War II, where he had honed the ability to rapidly assess a developing situation and make quick decisions in combat. **Lieutenant-Colonel Albert Crahay** commanded the Belgian battalion attached to 29th Brigade. Crahay had served in the Belgian Army prior to World War II, but was captured and held as a prisoner of war after the German invasion of 1940. An artilleryman by training, Crahay was a dashing figure who wore a silk scarf and had volunteered to command the Belgian battalion, even though it meant that he would have to give up command of an artillery regiment.

Like their Chinese opponents, the UN officers who defended the south bank of the Imjin in April 1951 were experienced and combat-proved leaders. However, the coming battle would test the mettle of both sides.

OPPOSING FORCES

CHINESE FORCES

Although they were called the Chinese People's Volunteer Army, CPVA members were not volunteers in the sense that they all chose to fight in Korea in some 'unofficial' way. This designation was intended to provide the Chinese government with plausible deniability to disguise the extent of Chinese involvement in the war. Consequently, the soldiers sent to fight in Korea were members of the regular army – the People's Liberation Army (PLA). Many soldiers, like their commanders, were battle-hardened veterans of wars against the Japanese (1937–45) and Nationalist Chinese (1945–49). Some, in fact, were former Nationalists who had been captured and subsequently joined the communist ranks. Others were communists from Mongolia and the former Japanese colony of Manchukuo (contemporary Manchuria). A few thousand military advisers from the Soviet Union were also assigned to the PLA.

The largest manoeuvre organization was the Army Group, which consisted of between two and six armies. Each Army comprised three divisions totalling 21,000–30,000 troops. Although a CPVA army is often considered the equivalent of a corps on the UN side, CPVA armies were actually only about one-and-a-half times the size of a single US or ROK division. Likewise, Chinese divisions were smaller than their UN counterparts. Numbering between 7,000 and 10,000 soldiers, a CPVA division was approximately two-thirds the size of a typical US or ROK division. Chinese divisions consisted of three regiments of 3,000–3,400 men. A regiment was responsible for three battalions of three companies each.

Discipline was based primarily on political indoctrination and public shaming. As in other communist militaries, Chinese units had political commissars

North Korean troops learn how to operate a Soviet-made light machine gun. Both Chinese and North Korean forces were equipped predominantly with Soviet weapons. (Sovfoto/UIG via Getty Images)

Chinese troops wore sand-coloured uniforms and soft caps into battle. (Sovfoto/UIG via Getty Images)

embedded at all levels of command to ensure that soldiers' words and deeds remained in line with the dictates of the Chinese Communist Party. Commissars taught political classes to spread communist messages and monitored soldiers' morale. Public shaming was used as a negative form of punishment when soldiers failed to obey orders.

The Chinese army was predominantly an infantry force that had little in the way of motorized transportation. For this reason, Chinese soldiers largely travelled on foot. They also travelled lightly, carrying a bandolier with a seven-day ration of rice. In terms of uniforms and personal equipment, they wore light, sand-coloured cotton uniforms during the spring and summer months and had quilted jackets to wear during the winter. Most wore soft caps rather than helmets. Standard-issue footwear consisted of rubber-soled canvas shoes for use during warm weather rather than the leather combat boots that were the mainstay of Western armies. These shoes were not as rugged as heavy leather boots, but were quieter when patrolling in dense brush. Initially equipped with an assortment of Soviet-made weapons and European or American-manufactured arms captured from the Nationalists, by spring 1951 the CPVA had begun to receive significantly more Soviet equipment. Although the bulk of this equipment did not arrive from Soviet stockpiles until after the Chinese offensive had begun, the CPVA of spring 1951 was better equipped than it had been when it entered Korea the previous year.

Chinese tactics reflected the strengths of this lightly equipped, infantry-centric force. Commanders relied on speed and infiltration on foot over rough terrain to attack the flanks and rear of enemy units. The idea was to surround enemy forces and annihilate them through close combat. Chinese forces preferred to conduct extensive reconnaissance of enemy positions prior to attacking them, often launching one or two probing attacks designed to test enemy defences and identify weak points. The CPVA regularly attacked at night, which allowed them to minimize UN firepower advantages, infiltrate

UN lines and sneak close to UN defences before engaging at short ranges with small arms and grenades. Machine guns and mortars would concentrate their fire on UN strongpoints, facilitating infantry assaults by suppressing UN defenders. Such infantry assaults often took the form of a human wave in which troops would infiltrate in small units, concentrate at an assembly area as close to their objective as possible – the base of a hill, for instance – then rush towards the enemy position en masse. Ideally, commanders were supposed to coordinate these assaults so that simultaneous attacks would land at different points of the enemy front line. The shock and confusion of suddenly facing swarms of Chinese troops rushing forward at close range proved overwhelming during the first months of the Chinese intervention.

In many ways, Chinese forces remained at a technological disadvantage when compared with their UN opponents. For example, while UN units relied on radios for communication at all levels, radios were in scant supply for the CPVA. For tactical-level communication in battle, Chinese troops used bugles to coordinate company-level instructions and whistles for platoon-level orders. Occasionally, Chinese forces employed gongs as well. In terms of logistics, Chinese forces had trucks at their disposal, but these were in short supply. Many units had to rely on pack animals, carts and human porters to carry their heavy equipment. Although the CPVA was equipped with tanks and artillery, these assets were limited in number. Most Chinese units relied on light mortars and machine guns for fire support. Against UN tanks, Chinese soldiers used satchel charges, explosives mounted on a pole (called pole charges), or sticky bombs designed to adhere to the side of an armoured vehicle. All of these anti-tank weapons required soldiers to engage UN tanks at point-blank range – a difficult and dangerous task.

The most obvious technological disadvantage was the Chinese lack of airpower. The CPVA largely had to rely on air assets provided by the Soviet Union. The Soviet Air Force deployed two fighter divisions that flew air-to-air missions in support of Chinese and North Korean forces, but disguised their aircraft using Chinese markings. Soviet fighters and several additional Soviet anti-aircraft units defended the strategically vital Yalu River crossing sites, but the Soviets refused to provide air cover over UN-controlled areas, out of concern that their involvement would be discovered. This decision left front-line Chinese ground forces vulnerable to UN airstrikes throughout the 1951 Spring Offensive.

Despite this disadvantage, Chinese forces adapted quickly. They routinely travelled at night because UN spotter aircraft could not see them, then hid in a concealed position during daylight hours before moving again at nightfall. Operational requirements meant that Chinese units could not always travel solely at night, so when moving during daylight hours, troops carried tree branches over their shoulders. When an aircraft was spotted, they would stop and bend down on one knee. From the air, the mass of soldiers would simply blend into the forest around them. This ruse and other forms of disguise helped Chinese forces avoid detection.

Against British troops, the Chinese were generally on par in terms of individual small arms. Each infantry company was armed with two medium machine guns, three light machine guns and a 60mm mortar. Although older designs left over from the wars against Japan and the Nationalist Chinese remained in service, many of these weapons were newer Soviet models. Individual soldiers were equipped with either a Soviet-made rifle or sub-machine gun, which UN troops nicknamed the 'burp gun'. The most popular design was the Type 50, a Chinese version of World War II era Soviet-made PPsh-41. This weapon had a higher rate of fire than British rifles and was more reliable than British sub-machine guns. About half of Chinese soldiers carried burp guns. Chinese infantry could therefore generate a higher volume of fire than their British opponents, but Chinese ammunition supplies were more limited and had to be carried by hand across difficult terrain to keep up with the offensive. Chinese infantrymen also carried about four grenades per man. These Soviet-made 'stick' grenades were lightweight but relied on concussive power to kill or disable the enemy rather than fragmentation, which meant that Chinese grenades had a relatively small kill radius.

The greatest CPVA weakness was in logistics. In April prior to the offensive, Chinese forces had amassed 15,000 tons of food for the assault, but this stockpile was insufficient to meet operational requirements for the sheer number of soldiers involved. Besides, having enough supplies was only one part of the challenge – logistical units had to move these stockpiles quickly and over long distances in order to resupply forward units during the offensive. These long supply lines were easily interdicted by UN aircraft during daylight hours, so logistical units were limited to operating at night, which was more difficult and less efficient. Furthermore, ammunition was in short supply. Against 29th Brigade at the Imjin, ammunition shortages inhibited the Chinese small-arms advantage over British troops: Chinese infantrymen had the ability to fire more bullets than their British enemies, but they would run out of those bullets more quickly.

Although the CPVA was a battle-hardened force, many of the units involved in the 1951 Spring Offensive were new to operations in Korea. These troops had plenty of experience fighting Japanese and Nationalist Chinese, but their opponents fighting under the UN banner in Korea were far more technologically advanced and could call upon much more sophisticated transportation and logistical systems than the Japanese or Nationalists. These fresh Chinese troops would soon discover that their new adversaries presented a different kind of foe.

The terrain where companies and platoons dug in was often too difficult for supply trucks, so Korean porters carried supplies up steep hills to forward positions. (IWM, BF 434)

UN FORCES

Fighting forces came from 15 UN member states as well as South Korea, which was not a member of the United Nations at the time. In terms of ground troops, South Korea provided the largest contingent (the ROK Army), with the United States contributing the second-largest force. Although many ROK units were overwhelmed during the June 1950 North Korean invasion due to poor equipment and a training focus on internal security rather than conventional warfare against a modern opponent, the ROK Army improved dramatically over the course of the war. ROK forces were of uneven quality, however, with some units having suffered from terrible losses and shattered morale as a result of the Chinese intervention. Other units, such as the ROK 1st Division, which held the front immediately to the west of the British 29th Brigade during the battle of the Imjin River, were well-led crack troops known for their bravery. ROK units were equipped with American uniforms and weaponry and received most of their logistical support from US forces.

Logistics were a particular strength of the US Army. Although most American combat troops in Korea were dismounted infantrymen, US units had an extensive logistical system at their disposal. With a few exceptions, the plethora of American trucks and supply aircraft ensured that US and other UN forces almost always had access to ample supplies of food, water and ammunition. Cargo planes such as the C-119 Flying Boxcar were also frequently used to resupply isolated ground forces through airdrops. Several such airdrops were attempted during the Chinese 1951 Spring Offensive. Because of the United States' logistical capabilities, UN forces were generally well supplied, unlike their Chinese opponents.

The United States also conducted the majority of UN air operations. These operations included strategic bombing of North Korean industry and infrastructure as well as close air support for ground troops. Ground attack aircraft available to the UN included a mix of World War II era prop-driven airframes, such as the F-51D Mustang (formerly designated the P-51D), and first-generation jet aircraft such as the F-80C Shooting Star and F9F Panther. The armament on these aircraft varied, but generally included 5-inch rockets, 20mm cannons, .50-calibre machine guns and a bomb payload of 2,000–4,000 pounds. One of the most feared weapons that UN aircraft could deliver was napalm. Napalm consists of a chemical gelling agent and an incendiary fuel, such as gasoline. When ignited, the jelly substance sticks to clothing or exposed skin and burns at more than 800° Celsius (1,472°F) – hot enough to burn men alive. Loaded into large tanks and dropped from low-flying aircraft, this frightening concoction was a commonly used anti-personnel weapon. However, the Chinese were not entirely defenceless against napalm. Chinese soldiers learned that napalm jelly would not stick to them if they took cover underneath a waterproof groundsheet. Although this countermeasure meant that napalm did not always kill the Chinese who had to endure it, napalm strikes still disrupted Chinese movements by forcing them to stop and seek cover.

Some British soldiers, like the Royal Ulster Rifles captain depicted here, obtained American-made M1 carbines to make up for the Sten gun's poor quality. The semi-automatic M1 carbine was lightweight and fitted with either a 15- or 30-round detachable magazine. (Dan Green, Novus Studios)

Britain and the Commonwealth provided the third-largest contingent to the UN war effort. The unit involved at the Imjin River was 29th Brigade – officially titled the 29th Independent Infantry Brigade Group. Based in Colchester, 29th Brigade was the second Commonwealth brigade to arrive in Korea. The first, 27th Brigade, consisted of British, Australian, Canadian and New Zealand troops. 29th Brigade, however, was raised entirely from units based in the United Kingdom. When it departed Britain for Korea in October 1950, 29th Brigade consisted of three infantry battalions, a tank regiment, an artillery regiment, an independent heavy mortar battery and a light anti-aircraft battery.

The infantry battalions under 29th Brigade all came from distinguished regiments. The oldest, raised in 1674, was the 1st Battalion, Royal Northumberland Fusiliers. During World War II, the battalion had served in North Africa, Sicily and Italy. The regiment was a close-knit organization that mainly recruited from north-east England, with many soldiers coming from industrial or mining backgrounds.

The next infantry battalion – 1st Battalion, the Gloucestershire Regiment ('Glosters') – was raised in 1694 and had more battle honours than any other regiment in the army. All British regiments have distinctive cap badges worn on the front of the soldiers' headgear, but the Glosters were unique in that they were permitted to wear a back badge as well. This honour was awarded to them after an action in Alexandria during 1801 when their French adversaries attacked the regiment from the front and rear. The rear rank simply performed an about-face, allowing the men to fight back-to-back. The story of the back badge was a key aspect of Gloster heritage and an important source of pride in the unit.

The third of 29th Brigade's infantry battalions was also the youngest. Formed in 1793, 1st Battalion, the Royal Ulster Rifles was trained as a glider infantry unit during World War II and fought in Normandy as well as the Battle of the Bulge, among other campaigns. The Rifles were considered an elite unit. Many of the men were of Irish descent, and the regiment recruited both Protestants and Catholics from within Northern Ireland and the Republic.

These battalions formed the core of 29th Brigade's fighting force. They were manned with a mix of regulars who had volunteered to fight in Korea and reservists called up to active service. The men were a combination of inexperienced recruits and grizzled veterans. Many were also conscripts, brought into the army as a result of the 1948 National Service Act, which was intended to bolster the ranks of the military in response to the emergence of the Cold War.

On paper, the official strength of an infantry battalion in the British Army was 38 officers and 945 other ranks. Most battalions in Korea were actually manned at lower strength, usually between 750 and 800 men. The battalion comprised four rifle companies, a headquarters company and a support company (heavy weapons and engineers). Officially, each infantry company had 130 men sub-divided into three platoons of 35 each as well as a small headquarters element. Each platoon consisted of a small headquarters section and three rifle sections of ten men. The support company had six 3-inch mortars, six Vickers medium machine guns (originally introduced

The Glosters' back badge, which commemorate the battle of Alexandria, 21 March 1801, when the 28th (North Gloucestershire) Regiment was attacked by the French from both front and rear and had to fight back-to-back. (IWM, INS 5714)

23

Men of the Gloucestershire Regiment, the Royal Engineers and the Royal Armoured Corps board the SS *Empire Windrush* at Southampton, bound for Korea. (Keystone/Getty Images)

in 1912, but solid and reliable), a sapper platoon (combat engineers), and an anti-tank section armed with towed anti-tank guns and Oxford carriers. Oxford carriers were similar to their more famous cousin, the Bren carrier, but were larger, more mobile, and could carry up to ten soldiers. By the time 29th Brigade arrived in Korea, North Korean armoured forces had been annihilated. Without an enemy tank threat, the anti-tank guns were useless, so 29th Brigade left them behind, but continued to use the Oxford carriers as armoured utility vehicles to move soldiers and equipment around the battlefield.

Most of the individual British soldier's equipment would have been familiar to a veteran of World War II. The 1914- or 1944-pattern steel 'Tommy' helmet was standard issue, but soldiers almost universally chose not to wear them. The helmets were bulky and, without much threat of enemy artillery bombardment, British troops preferred to march and fight while wearing regimental berets or soft, wool cap comforters. In terms of weaponry, the standard infantry weapon was the .303-calibre Lee-Enfield with a ten-round magazine. Because it was a bolt-action rifle, the firer had to raise his hand, pull the bolt back, then charge it forwards to load the next round. Although this process slowed the weapon's rate of fire, the Lee-Enfield was accurate and reliable. If not armed with a rifle, British infantrymen carried the 9mm Sten sub-machine gun. The Sten gun had a 32-round magazine, but could become extremely hot to the touch when fired for long periods during sustained engagements. It also had a slow rate of fire (550 rounds per minute) compared with other sub-machine guns and frequently jammed. In addition to the Lee-Enfield and Sten, each infantry section was armed with a Bren light machine gun. The Bren had a 30-round magazine that loaded from the top of the weapon, giving it a distinctive appearance. It was an old weapon with a relatively slow rate of fire (500 rounds per minute), but it was reliable. Officers were issued six-round, .38-calibre Webley revolvers, but most officers also chose to carry a Sten gun or Lee-Enfield because the revolver was ineffective except at point-blank range.

British soldiers were also issued with large numbers of grenades. The No. 36 fragmentation grenade, also known as the Mills Bomb, was intended as a defensive grenade. It had a large explosive charge and 35m-wide (38yd) blast radius. When defending hilltop positions, British troops often simply rolled grenades down the hill at oncoming Chinese infantry. Grenades were also excellent weapons for use at night. The reduced visibility of night fighting meant that tactical engagements were often decided at short ranges through close combat. British troops could listen for the sounds of advancing Chinese, then hurl a volley of grenades in their general direction. Thanks to the No. 36 grenade's large blast radius, a grenade-thrower's aim did not have to be precise.

In addition to infantry units, 29th Brigade included several other combat elements. The other Irish unit in the brigade was 8th King's Royal Irish Hussars. Originally formed as light cavalry, the regiment had participated in the charge of the light brigade during the Crimean War. It became a tank unit during the Second World War, where the regiment fought at Alamein and Normandy. Although the entire regiment – the headquarters and three tank squadrons – deployed to Korea, only C Squadron was with the brigade when the Chinese offensive began. C Squadron consisted of a headquarters section and four troops of four tanks each.

Although most of the brigade's equipment dated to World War II or earlier, that was not the case for the Hussars and their state-of-the-art Centurion Mk. III medium tanks. Armed with a 20-pounder cannon, the Hussars' Centurions were also equipped with gun stabilizer systems that allowed the tanks to fire accurately while on the move. Furthermore, the Centurion's heavy armour meant that the crew was well protected. The Centurion did have its disadvantages, however. At 50,000kg (50 tonnes), the Centurion was an unwieldy vehicle in tight spaces. The terrain in Korea – steep hillsides, poorly maintained roads, soggy rice paddies and numerous irrigation ditches – was difficult for tanks, but the Centurion's bulk further degraded its mobility. Additionally, the Centurion was only outfitted with one coaxial 7.92mm Besa machine gun. The lack of a pintle-mounted machine gun on top of the tank's turret restricted the Centurion to only being able to fire in one direction. American tanks, in contrast, were armed with three machine guns – one in the bow of the tank, one coaxial and one pintle-mounted machine gun on the turret. The lack of additional machine guns meant that Centurions were vulnerable to infantry attacks at close ranges, especially at night. As a result of this vulnerability, it was British standard procedure to withdraw tanks from the front lines at nightfall and form them in a tight, easily defended circle called a leaguer.

The Brigade also had attached engineer and artillery units. The sappers of 55 Field Squadron, Royal Engineers were useful for clearing or laying mines, blowing up bridges and building field-expedient defences. They could also fight as infantrymen when necessary. In terms of fire support, 45 Field Regiment, Royal Artillery was equipped with 25-pounder howitzers. British artillery was under-gunned compared with American artillery, but the

Issued in large quantities to British troops, fragmentation grenades proved their worth during defensive actions, especially at night. (Jean-Louis Dubois)

Although it was heavy and difficult to manoeuvre in confined spaces, the Centurion was well armoured and carried a powerful 20-pounder main gun. (IWM, BF 10299)

25-pounder was a reliable weapon with a high rate of fire (five rounds per minute). 45 Field Regiment was organized into three firing batteries of eight guns each, for a total of 24 guns. Forward observers embedded with each infantry battalion coordinated artillery fire during battle. In addition to howitzers, 29th Brigade could call upon the heavy, 4.2-inch mortars of 170 Independent Mortar Battery. The battery comprised three troops – one troop was assigned to support each infantry battalion. Finally, A Troop, 11 (Sphinx) Light Anti-Aircraft Battery was also assigned to the brigade. The anti-aircraft troops soon found that the brigade

American-made half-tracks and jeeps proved useful as utility vehicles. Jeeps were plentiful, but 29th Brigade only had a handful of half-tracks, many of which were used for casualty evacuation. (Korea, by Joan Wanklyn, Canadian War Museum)

had little need for them to serve in their primary role due to the lack of an enemy air threat, but 11 Battery adapted by using their 40mm Bofors anti-aircraft guns as anti-personnel weapons. They were often used to protect vulnerable rear areas, such as the brigade headquarters and artillery firing positions, from Chinese infiltration.

Less than two weeks before the battle at the Imjin River, 29th Brigade received reinforcements in the form of a fourth infantry battalion from Belgium. The unit was Belgium's contribution to the UN war effort, but also included a platoon from Luxembourg. Although the Belgian battalion was only about half the size of British infantry battalions, the Belgians were a stalwart unit of hard-fighting volunteers, many of whom were veterans of the Second World War. They wore British-style uniforms and equipment, but stood out from British forces by their green berets and relaxed grooming standards – many men wore beards.

ORDERS OF BATTLE

UN FORCES

3rd US Infantry Division (Maj. Gen. Robert Soule)

29th UK Independent Infantry Brigade Group (Brig. Tom Brodie)
    1st Battalion, Gloucestershire Regiment (Lt. Col. James Carne)
    1st Battalion, Royal Northumberland Fusiliers (Lt. Col. Kingsley Foster)
    1st Battalion, Royal Ulster Rifles (Maj. Gerald Rickord)
    Belgian Infantry Battalion (Lt. Col. Albert Crahay)
    C Squadron, 8th King's Royal Irish Hussars (Maj. Henry Huth)
    45 Field Regiment, Royal Artillery (Lt. Col. Maris Young)
    11 (Sphinx) Light Anti-Aircraft Battery (Maj. M.V.F. Fawkes)
    170 Independent Mortar Battery (Maj. T.Y. Fischer-Hoch)
    55 Field Squadron, Royal Engineers (Maj. Tony Younger)

CHINESE FORCES

XIX Army Group (Yang Dezhi)

63rd Army (Fu Chongbi)
    187th Division
        559th Regiment
        560th Regiment
        561st Regiment
    188th Division
        562nd Regiment
        563rd Regiment
        564th Regiment
    189th Division
        565th Regiment
        566th Regiment
        567th Regiment

OPPOSING PLANS

CHINESE PLANS

After sustaining heavy losses during their initial intervention and Eighth Army's subsequent counter-offensives, Mao and Peng recognized that a quick victory was not possible. Consequently, they began planning for a massive, decisive offensive in spring 1951. The concept of operations relied on numerical superiority to encircle and annihilate UN forces. Towards this end, Mao sent reinforcements to Korea. By mid-April 1951, Peng Dehuai had over 1.3 million soldiers at his disposal. The bulk of these forces were in combat units: 42 infantry divisions, eight artillery divisions and four anti-aircraft divisions totalling 770,000 troops. This massive force was organized into four army groups of 14 armies. In contrast, UN forces totalled only 340,000 men: Approximately 150,000 Americans, 130,000 ROK troops and 60,000 soldiers from other UN member states.
The Chinese had a three-to-one advantage.

By early 1951, the initial Chinese intervention had succeeded in recapturing most pre-war North Korean territory, but Chinese forces had sustained large numbers of casualties, including thousands of soldiers who were captured during UN counter-offensives, such as these men being escorted by Turkish troops. (Keystone/Getty Images)

The underlying concept of Peng's plan was to fix UN forces in the centre through attacks by III Army Group, with two pincers designed to penetrate UN lines and turn inwards, creating a double envelopment. The IX Army Group and XIII Army Group, which formed the eastern pincer, were instructed to penetrate as far south as the area around Kap'yong, thereby cutting off UN forces' east-west lines of communication in the process. This eastern pincer would then wheel to the west, turn US I Corps' eastern flank, and attack the US 24th and 25th Divisions. The Chinese main effort, however, lay with the western pincer – XIX Army Group. Peng directed XIX Army Group commander Yang Dezhi to strike I Corps' western flank, pushing through the Munsan and Uijeongbu corridors. South of the UN front line, the ground along these two corridors opens from constricted, mountainous terrain to wide, flat fields and roads that can accommodate the rapid movement of large armies. Both corridors had been used as invasion

Chinese Spring Offensive, Attack Plans in the Western Theatre

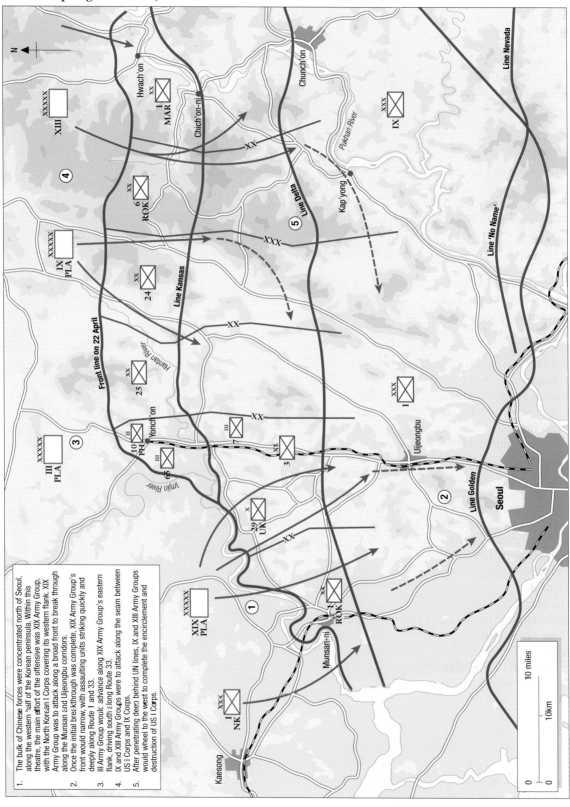

1. The bulk of Chinese forces were concentrated north of Seoul, along the western half of the Korean peninsula. Within this theatre, the main effort of the offensive was XIX Army Group, with the North Korean I Corps covering its western flank. XIX Army Group was to attack along a broad front to break through along the Munsan and Uijeongbu corridors.

2. Once the initial breakthrough was complete, XIX Army Group's front would narrow, with assaulting units striking quickly and deeply along Route 1 and 33.

3. III Army Group would advance along XIX Army Group's eastern flank, driving south along Route 33.

4. IX and XIII Army Groups were to attack along the seam between US I Corps and IX Corps.

5. After penetrating deep behind UN lines, IX and XIII Army Groups would wheel to the west to complete the encirclement and destruction of US I Corps.

routes for centuries prior to the Korean War. If successful, the two Chinese pincers would encircle much of I Corps and open the path to Seoul.

Comprising the 63rd, 64th and 65th Armies, XIX Army Group was part of the recent wave of reinforcements that Mao had despatched to Korea specifically to take part in the Spring Offensive. XIX Army Group's objectives were twofold: capture Uijeongbu to open the route to Seoul and, secondly, destroy several UN combat units (ROK 1st Division, US 3rd Division, British 29th Brigade and the Turkish Brigade). The 64th Army was to attack ROK 1st Division while 63rd Army severed the 29th Brigade from the rest of the US 3rd Division. Mao wanted to completely annihilate an enemy brigade or division in every major engagement. He believed that it was more effective to eliminate one entire unit than to defeat ten. His emphasis on the annihilation of entire units was manifested in Chinese tactics,

In preparation for the offensive, Chinese soldiers carried seven days' worth of rice rations in horseshoe-shaped tubes like this. The other bag in the photograph is a grenade carrier for two 'stick' grenades. (IWM, EQU 4233)

which sought to fix the enemy in position, encircle them, and then destroy them in place.

The Chinese plan relied on numerical superiority and fighting spirit to overcome the UN forces' firepower and technological advantages. But the large number of Chinese soldiers involved in the offensive meant that logistical services had to supply more food, water and ammunition for front-line troops. Command and control was also more difficult, as regiments, divisions and armies had to transmit orders and reports across vast distances without much of the communications technology available to UN units. Furthermore, UN firepower and technological advantages allowed UN forces to interdict Chinese supply lines with air strikes and artillery bombardment. Considering these difficulties, several of Peng's subordinates disagreed with the plan. They advocated drawing UN forces further north, thus extending their supply lines and exposing them to encirclement. Peng overruled these objections – he refused to allow the Chinese to cede the initiative to UN forces.

Initially, Peng planned to begin the offensive in May, but the 'fog of war' intervened. In March 1951, Peng received intelligence suggesting that UN forces intended to launch an Inch'on-style amphibious assault on North Korea. This assessment was based on the presence of two US infantry divisions that had arrived in Japan. Chinese intelligence, however, was incorrect. The two divisions were not being kept in Japan as a prelude to an amphibious assault; instead, they were held as a reserve in the event that the Soviet Union intervened in the war. However, this incorrect intelligence assessment convinced Peng to launch the offensive as quickly as possible.

One of the Glosters' first actions against the Chinese was a March 1951 assault on Hill 327, supported by Centurion tanks. The Glosters faced a small Chinese rear-guard element, which fled soon after the attack began. (IWM, BF 454)

With many units still in transit to their staging areas and still unfamiliar with the terrain in which they would be operating, Peng determined that mid-April was the earliest that he could initiate the offensive.

There was a problem with moving the date of the offensive forward by one month: III and XIX Army Groups were not ready. Many soldiers had not reached their staging areas by 22 April, when the offensive was supposed to begin. This was particularly true of 64th Army. When the 64th Army commander realized this and called Yang at XIX Army Group headquarters to ask for more time, Yang simply hung up the phone – the answer, apparently, was 'no'. The 64th Army's front-line divisions had to run 16–24km (10–15 miles) to their staging areas to begin the assault on time. Consequently, they were already exhausted when the offensive began. The men of 63rd Army, who would face 29th Brigade, were in better shape because they had been encamped behind the front line since mid-March. They would need all of their strength in the fight to come.

UN PLANS

By 22 April, UN forces occupied Line Kansas, with the exception of the northward salient created by Operation *Dauntless*. The salient was 64km (40 miles) wide and 16km (10 miles) deep at its greatest point. It ran from the Hwacheon Reservoir in the east to the 'hinge' where the course of the Imjin River turns from north–south to east–west. Operation *Dauntless* was still underway, with Gen. Van Fleet continuing to push I Corps and IX Corps towards their objectives along Lines Utah and Wyoming. The British 29th Brigade, attached to the US 3rd Division of US I Corps, occupied the line south of the hinge. ROK 1st Division held the ground to 29th Brigade's left, while the remainder of US 3rd Division occupied the hinge and the most westerly part of Line Utah, to 29th Brigade's immediate right flank. The rest of I Corps lay to US 3rd Division's right: the Turkish Brigade, US 25th Division and US 24th Division, respectively. IX Corps was east of I Corps, followed by X Corps, ROK III Corps and ROK I Corps on Korea's east coast.

Throughout the month of April, there was little action in 29th Brigade's sector. In fact, between 11 and 20 April, Chinese activity was notable by its absence. British patrols across the Imjin encountered small detachments of Chinese soldiers, but found little evidence of major enemy movements near the front line. Comprising Centurion tanks and dismounted infantry, British patrols dominated the Imjin's northern bank during daylight hours, but the Chinese owned the night. Chinese troops dug tunnels into hillsides on the north side of the river where they could shelter without being seen from the air. They could also hide in the tunnels during daylight hours so that British patrols would not find them. The Chinese were massing forces quietly and largely unseen by the British. Although front line units

Before they were replaced by the Belgians, the Royal Ulster Rifles dug entrenchments, laid barbed wire, and prepared minefields on the approaches to Hill 194. It was the only 29th Brigade position that was heavily fortified when the battle began on 22 April. (IWM, BF 224)

had not discovered signs of the impending offensive, UN reconnaissance aircraft had noticed significant enemy activity further to the north. These observations and other reports had led Eighth Army intelligence officers to determine that a Chinese offensive would begin soon, most likely between 20 April and 1 May.

UN commanders recognized that a Chinese offensive would most likely strike ROK 1st Division, 29th Brigade and US 3rd Division because these units held a key segment of the front line. ROK 1st Division held positions along the Munsan corridor, while US 3rd Division occupied the Uijeongbu corridor. 29th Brigade held a line of hills in between the Munsan and Uijeongbu corridors. The ability to hold these positions, or at least slow a potential Chinese offensive to prevent a quick breakthrough, was vital to the UN war effort. For 29th Brigade, holding the bend in the Imjin River would prevent the defenders of the Munsan and Uijeongbu corridors from being outflanked.

However, 29th Brigade's assigned sector of the front was wider than that normally assigned to a brigade-sized unit. British brigades were often assigned wider fronts than other UN forces because they had more soldiers than a typical American regimental combat team. American commanders also viewed British troops as highly skilled, tough and reliable in difficult situations, so many men of 29th Brigade came to view the fact that they were regularly assigned to wide fronts as a point of honour. The disadvantage of occupying larger swathes of territory was that British units were frequently

The bend in the Imjin River, as seen from the south bank. (IWM, BF 10278)

more dispersed than other UN forces, which could make them more vulnerable to infiltration. Along the Imjin, 29th Brigade held 14km (9 miles) of front by straight-line distance, but in actuality, the brigade had to secure about 23km (14 miles) due to the curve of the river – a frontage better suited to a division-sized unit rather than an entire brigade.

Brigadier Brodie deployed three of his four infantry battalions on the front line, with the Royal Ulster Rifles in reserve along with the Hussar squadron and the artillery. In the east, north of the Imjin, the Belgian battalion occupied Hill 194. This position protected the flank of the US 65th Infantry Regiment, which secured the main supply route, Route 33, to the east of 29th Brigade's sector. Two pontoon bridges lay to the south of Hill 194 at a site called Ulster Crossing – one bridge crossed the Imjin at the point where the river turns 90 degrees to the north, while the second bridge crossed the Hantan River, a tributary of the Imjin, to the east of the first bridge. These bridges connected the Hill 194 position with the remainder of the brigade to the south of the Imjin.

South-west of the Belgians, in the centre of the brigade's line, the Royal Northumberland Fusiliers secured hilltop positions between the Imjin and a secondary road named Route 11. Each Fusilier company occupied a hilltop or ridgeline overlooking the river, with the exception of Y Company, which was deployed along the river bank. To the west of the Northumberlands, the Glosters secured the brigade's left flank. Lieutenant-Colonel Carne deployed his battalion so that it straddled Route 5Y, a dirt road that crossed the Imjin at a ford known as Gloster Crossing. Three companies held the foothills of the 675m -high (2,215ft) mountain called Kamaksan, while the fourth company occupied Hill 148, nicknamed 'Castle Site' after the ancient ruins found there. Hill 148 lay

west of Route 5Y and overlooked the Imjin. ROK 1st Division held the ground to the west of the Glosters, but the closest ROK position was over a mile away from the Glosters.

The hills and ridges of the area were steep and rocky. Trees and bushes grew along the slopes and crests. The two roads in 29th Brigade's sector – Route 5Y and Route 11 – ran generally south from the river on either side of Kamaksan. East of the mountain, Route 11 ran north–south in a flat, open valley several hundred metres wide, with rocky heights running parallel to the road. Farmhouses dotted the valley intermittently, and the small village

of Hwangbang-ni lay near the point where Route 11 traversed a small rise 50–100 metres (54–108 yards) higher in elevation than the rest of the valley. This saddle marked the southern entrance to the valley. Route 5Y ran along the floor of another, narrower valley to the west of Kamaksan before exiting the valley and merging with Route 11. Route 11 continued an additional 5km (3 miles) to the south-east before intersecting with Route 33.

This was difficult terrain in which to fight. Routes 11 and 5Y were unimproved roads, but were passable. In the valleys, nearly every flat strip of land had been converted into a rice paddy. The rice crop had not yet been planted, so the paddies were not filled with water, but the ground was still soft. Each rectangular paddy field was also demarcated with earthen walls or mounds, and surrounded by a network of drainage ditches – the kind of terrain that made mechanized manoeuvres particularly challenging. For the infantry, digging entrenchments also proved challenging. The sharp rocks and steep hillsides made the preparation of fighting positions a back-breaking task. Most troops dug small two-man trenches and piled rocks in front, but few bothered to lay mines, barbed wire or other obstacles on the approaches to their positions. The men were still of the mindset that they would soon be advancing again. However, Hill 194 was well fortified with mines and wire obstacles because the Ulsters, who had originally occupied it, felt exposed and vulnerable with the Imjin and Hantan Rivers behind them. When the Chinese offensive began, the Belgians, who had recently replaced the Ulsters on Hill 194, had reason to be thankful for these fortifications.

THE BATTLE OF THE IMJIN RIVER

DAY 1: SUNDAY, 22 APRIL

Sunday, 22 April began as a quiet day for the men of 29th Brigade. Some soldiers attended church services or enjoyed the clear, comfortable spring weather. The Northumberland Fusiliers prepared for their annual regimental St George's Day celebration to be held the following day. Despite the relaxed attitude within the brigade, reconnaissance patrols encountered Chinese troops north of the river. Several patrols engaged in brief skirmishes with squad- and platoon-sized Chinese units. By evening, Korean civilians fleeing to the south reported that they too had seen large numbers of Chinese soldiers marching south. Meanwhile, UN aircraft spotted hundreds of Chinese troops and artillery heading south.

Brigadier Brodie and his superiors at division and corps headquarters therefore expected a fight, but because intelligence suggested that the main Chinese force remained about 32km (20 miles) away, UN commanders only anticipated facing probing attacks on the night of 22 April. Still, Brodie

Returning from a patrol on the north bank of the Imjin River, Fusiliers ride on a Centurion tank from 8th King's Royal Irish Hussars as it climbs the riverbank. (IWM, BF 10317)

Initial Chinese Attacks on 29th Brigade Positions, 22–23 April

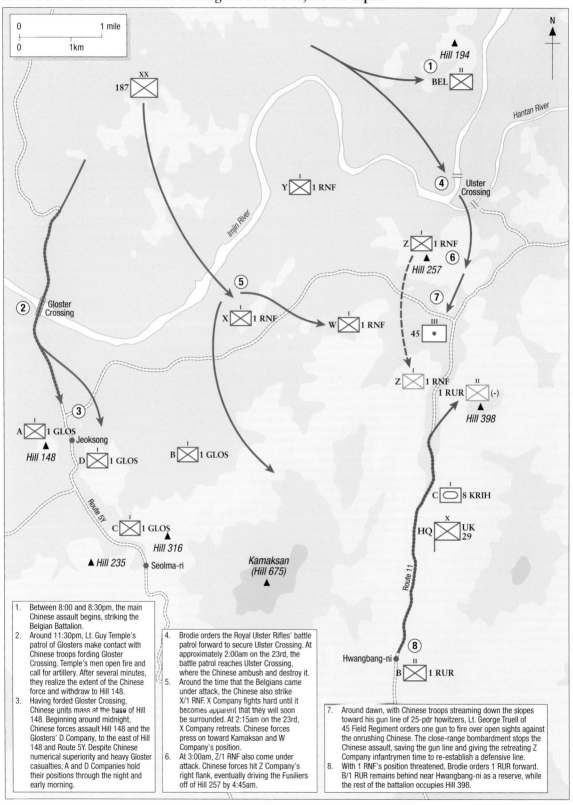

1. Between 8:00 and 8:30pm, the main Chinese assault begins, striking the Belgian Battalion.
2. Around 11:30pm, Lt. Guy Temple's patrol of Glosters make contact with Chinese troops fording Gloster Crossing. Temple's men open fire and call for artillery. After several minutes, they realize the extent of the Chinese force and withdraw to Hill 148.
3. Having forded Gloster Crossing, Chinese units mass at the base of Hill 148. Beginning around midnight, Chinese forces assault Hill 148 and the Glosters' D Company, to the east of Hill 148 and Route 5Y. Despite Chinese numerical superiority and heavy Gloster casualties, A and D Companies hold their positions through the night and early morning.

4. Brodie orders the Royal Ulster Rifles' battle patrol forward to secure Ulster Crossing. At approximately 2:00am on the 23rd, the battle patrol reaches Ulster Crossing, where the Chinese ambush and destroy it.
5. Around the time that the Belgians came under attack, the Chinese also strike X/1 RNF. X Company fights hard until it becomes apparent that they will soon be surrounded. At 2:15am on the 23rd, X Company retreats. Chinese forces press on toward Kamaksan and W Company's position.
6. At 3:00am, Z/1 RNF also come under attack. Chinese forces hit Z Company's right flank, eventually driving the Fusiliers off of Hill 257 by 4:45am.

7. Around dawn, with Chinese troops streaming down the slopes toward his gun line of 25-pdr howitzers, Lt. George Truell of 45 Field Regiment orders one gun to fire over open sights against the onrushing Chinese. The close-range bombardment stops the Chinese assault, saving the gun line and giving the retreating Z Company infantrymen time to re-establish a defensive line.
8. With 1 RNF's position threatened, Brodie orders 1 RUR forward. B/1 RUR remains behind near Hwangbang-ni as a reserve, while the rest of the battalion occupies Hill 398.

A Belgian machine-gun crew prepares for action. Despite their somewhat ragged appearance, the Belgians were excellent fighters. (IWM, MH 32791)

ordered that preparations be made. The brigade was put on 50 per cent stand-to, meaning that half of the troops could rest while the other half remained in their slit trenches. He also ordered the Ulsters, as the brigade reserve, to prepare a 'battle patrol' of 50 men in eight Oxford carriers as a quick reaction force ready to respond within 30 minutes of receiving orders.

The Battle Begins

The unit leading the Chinese offensive against 29th Brigade was the 187th Division of 63rd Army, supported by the 188th and 189th Divisions. Between 8.00 and 8.30pm, the lead Chinese elements smashed into the Belgian and Fusilier defences. The Belgians called for artillery and mortar fire. Combined with the barbed wire obstacles and land mines in front of their lines, the bombardment stalled the Chinese attack as the Belgians furiously defended their positions. By 11.00pm, units across the entire brigade front were in action. Based on the north side of the river, the Belgians were in the most vulnerable position. To prevent the Belgians from being cut off, Brodie ordered Maj. Gerald Rickord to send the Ulsters' battle patrol forward. They were to seize the bridges at Ulster Crossing that linked the Belgian position north of the Imjin with the rest of the brigade on the south bank.

On Hill 194, the Belgians heard the bugle calls that the Chinese used to signal the advance. The battalion's C Company bore the brunt of the initial Chinese attack. Belgian forward observers called for star shells to illuminate the ground in front of them. As the shells burst high in the air, Belgian troops saw that the entire northern bank of the river and much of the river itself was covered with Chinese soldiers. The Belgians poured rifle and machine-gun fire into the advancing Chinese and called in artillery fire from the overworked 45 Field Regiment howitzers. In the forward-most of C Company's positions, B Platoon began to run out of ammunition. Chinese troops had started to infiltrate B Platoon's defences, placing a machine gun in between two of the platoon's trench lines. The Belgians responded by destroying the machine gun nest with a bazooka round. At this point, the Chinese had broken through

Private First Class Frans Louis Clevis, of the Belgian battalion, watches his sector from a trench. Note the fragmentation grenades to his left. (IWM, MH 32814)

their lines, the platoon commander had been seriously wounded, and the second-in-command, Sgt. Armand Philips, had suffered a bullet wound in his jaw. Facing an increasingly desperate situation, Philips ordered B Platoon to link up with the rest of the company further to the rear. Miraculously, the entire platoon survived to re-join C Company. While Sgt. Philips extricated his troops, the rest of the Belgian battalion came under attack. Lieutenant-Colonel Crahay worried that the battalion might be cut off. He did not know that the Royal Ulster Rifles' battle patrol had been ordered to secure the bridges that the Belgians depended upon as a withdrawal route until he saw gunfire and explosions from the battle patrol's firefight.

Around 2.00am on the 23rd, the battle patrol reached Ulster Crossing and rumbled across. However, when they reached the north bank the Chinese ambushed them with a hail of fire that destroyed several Oxfords. Pinned down and exposed, the commander of the battle patrol, Lt. Hedley Craig, gathered a small group of Riflemen to cover the others as they retreated across the bridge. Only one Oxford and 27 soldiers returned. In addition to the terrible toll of casualties, the battle patrol had failed to secure the pontoon bridges that connected the Belgians with the rest of the brigade. The Belgians were isolated.

In the Glosters' sector, Lt. Col. Carne despatched a fighting patrol of 16 men to the river bank at Gloster Crossing. Around 11.30pm, the fighting patrol heard Chinese troops crossing the river and opened fire. As the number of Chinese troops crossing the river grew to brigade size, Carne realized he would have to pull the fighting patrol back and prepare for a general engagement. However, the Glosters were not the most hard-pressed British battalion at that point in the night.

Assault on the Northumberland Fusiliers

Between the Gloster and Belgian positions, the Royal Northumberland Fusiliers' X Company also came under attack. A listening post heard the oncoming Chinese infantry and, after reporting the Chinese movements, ran as fast as they could to return to X Company's lines. The Chinese came running immediately behind them, throwing grenades and firing rifles and burp guns at the nearest X Company position, which was 4 Platoon's. The platoon commander, Lt. Malcolm Cubiss, ordered his men to stand their ground. Fusiliers began to time their grenade throws so that the grenades would explode in the air above the attacking Chinese, the idea being that airburst explosions would spread the shrapnel out over a larger area and kill or wound more Chinese. But after three hours of fighting in which 4 Platoon suffered 14 killed out of 26 men in the unit, the Fusiliers were exhausted. Fearing that they might be surrounded and overrun, 4 Platoon retreated.

The Chinese used probing attacks to ascertain the location of British trenches and machine-gun positions, then set up machine guns of their own to provide covering fire as they advanced. Machine-gun tracer rounds also

served to mark the British positions for the main attacking force. As the attackers would close in on the British trench lines, they would stop about 18m (20 yards) short of the British, dig hasty 'shell scrapes' for cover, throw grenades, then assault by charging and firing burp guns. These tactics had driven 4 Platoon back, with the rest of X Company to follow.

X Company, like the other Fusilier companies, was vulnerable to night-time encirclement. None of the flanks of the Fusiliers' company positions were tied in with adjacent companies. Instead, each company occupied a separate hilltop. These positions could support each other in daylight, when Vickers machine guns sited in one company position could provide fire support to the others by covering the approaches to the flanks and rear of the other company positions. This was possible due to the Vickers' long range. At night, however, the Vickers gunners could not see well enough and cover the approaches, even with the advantage of star shells. There were simply too many Chinese and too much space in the bushes and folds of the ground for British gunners to identify and lay enough accurate fire onto the Chinese as they sought to encircle the isolated British defences. Furthermore, the Chinese were also able to infiltrate into X Company's sector through an unexpected avenue of approach. Chinese reconnaissance patrols had previously identified a ford in the Imjin near X Company's position that the British did not know existed. Using this ford, Chinese troops were able to cross the river in front of X Company largely unmolested by the kind of British artillery and mortar barrages that fell on the Chinese soldiers attacking the Belgian battalion. Consequently, the Chinese were able to assault X Company from several directions simultaneously.

Now facing the threat of X Company being surrounded and overrun, Fusilier battalion commander Lt. Col. Foster received permission from Brig. Brodie at 2.15am for X Company to retreat. At 2.45am, X Company fell back. However, the Chinese had already cut X Company off from the battalion headquarters, so the fleeing Fusiliers had to fight their way through Chinese troops that were swarming in the other direction. As one group

Sporting their berets and back badges, Glosters occupy a defensive position in what was likely a staged photograph. Lee-Enfield rifles and Sten guns were standard issue for British infantrymen; the ability to use those weapons proficiently was vital to the battalion's defence along the Imjin. (Popperfoto/ Getty Images)

of Fusiliers ran down from the hilltop, they noticed hundreds of Chinese soldiers crouched in a rice paddy at the bottom of the hill. Apparently waiting for orders, the Chinese were simply milling around and did not realize the handful of British soldiers had almost run into their midst. Wary of alerting the Chinese to their presence, the Fusiliers silently skirted the rice paddy as they crept slowly in the dark to the south-east.

X Company was not the only one of Lt. Col. Foster's companies that was in trouble. On Hill 257, the men of Z Company did not expect to be attacked without warning. They were located on a dominant terrain feature over a kilometre behind Y Company's position. The Z Company defences also overlooked the Imjin at a point that could not be forded. By the early morning of 23 April, Z Company could see the battle developing around them. They knew that X Company and the Belgian battalion were engaged, but so far had seen no evidence of Chinese troops preparing to attack their position – Z Company had not encountered any Chinese probing attacks or a preparatory mortar barrage. Shortly after 3.00am on the 23rd, however, Chinese troops struck Z Company's right flank, seemingly out of nowhere. The men of 11 Platoon, who held Z Company's right flank, did not know that the Ulsters' battle patrol had been decimated and the pontoon bridges between their position and the Belgians had been lost. Chinese troops were able to cross the bridges and mass silently below Z Company's position without being seen.

Z Company first realized that they were under attack when a few Chinese troops stepped across the tripwires that the Fusiliers had placed on the slopes of the hill. Attached to grenades that would go off when tripped, these booby traps exploded, killing several Chinese and warning Z Company of the impending danger. The Fusiliers fired at the oncoming Chinese, but their advance was so swift that a battalion-sized element swept into Z Company's positions. However, the Chinese avoided direct assaults on Z Company's slit trenches. Rather than seizing the hill, this first wave pushed through and beyond the Z Company defences. Their mission was to infiltrate and continue the advance into the valley beyond Hill 257. From here, they could reach Route 11 and potentially cut 29th Brigade in two.

Z Company's position was untenable. At 4.45am, the company retreated. The path to Route 11 and the valley was now open to the Chinese. Hundreds of Chinese soldiers streamed down from Hill 257. Situated in the valley less than a mile away was a major prize – the guns of 45 Field Regiment. If the Chinese reached the valley floor, they would overrun the guns that were providing vital fire support to the infantry battalions along the river bank. Fortunately for the British, a 45 Field Regiment officer, Lt. George Truell, recognized the danger. He deployed two Bren guns on his flank to cover Z Company's withdrawal. Once Z Company had retreated from the hill, Truell ordered one of his 25-pounders to engage the Chinese directly. He could only afford to turn one gun because of the need to continue firing in support of the infantry battalions. The 25-pounders had spent the entire night supporting the infantry using indirect fire, in which they relied on map coordinates and directions from forward observers co-located with the infantry. By ordering one gun to engage the Chinese infantry massing in front of him, Truell had to use his howitzer the old-fashioned way – lowering the gun tube and firing directly at the Chinese infantry. For 20 minutes, Truell's lone gun crew fired several high explosive shells at roughly 140 metres' (150 yards') distance – point-blank range by artillery standards. The fire was devastating. Dozens of Chinese troops were killed as the rest scattered for cover. Truell then despatched a patrol towards the Chinese position to clear the area. With the attack defeated and an infantry patrol in place, Truell had bought precious time for the brigade to regroup.

Lieutenants Philip Curtis (left) and Terry Waters (right) stand in front of an abandoned Buddhist temple near Hill 148. Curtis would later posthumously receive the Victoria Cross for his actions during the battle. (Soldiers of Gloucestershire Museum)

The Defence of Castle Site

As the Fusiliers were overrun and Truell's heroics prevented a disastrous breakthrough, the Glosters' forward companies on the brigade's left flank also fought through the night. The Glosters' A Company, occupying Hill 148, Castle Site, was the first Gloster unit attacked after the fighting patrol that had been despatched to Gloster Crossing. Around midnight, the Chinese struck A Company's 2 and 3 Platoons, on the slope facing the Imjin. The Glosters rolled grenades down the hill, opened fire with their rifles and Bren guns and immediately called for artillery support. Heavy machine-gun fire, from A and D Company Vickers guns that had been sited to provide interlocking fires, also helped to keep the Chinese at bay for a while, but the sheer number of attackers took its toll. A Chinese machine gun had managed to slip between the Gloster defences and occupied a bunker near the top of the hill. From this position, the Chinese poured effective fire on the paths

'CROSSING THE IMJIN' – THE CHINESE 187TH DIVISION ASSAULTS GLOSTER CROSSING, 11.30PM, 22 APRIL 1951 (PP. 42–43)

Chinese troops were under pressure to advance quickly in order to secure the southern bank of the Imjin. This move would allow follow-on forces to continue the assault on the Glosters' A Company, located on Hill 148. Early in the evening, the Glosters' commanding officer Lt. Col. Carne despatched a 'fighting patrol' of 16 men to the riverbank at Gloster Crossing to provide early warning in the event of a Chinese attack. Carne ordered the leader of the fighting patrol, Lt. Guy Temple, that, if possible, he was to capture an enemy prisoner for interrogation. Furthermore, Carne told Temple that if he encountered a small force, he was to ambush it. But if Chinese troops outnumbered his, Temple was supposed to withdraw. Armed with extra Bren gun ammunition and transported by Oxford carriers, Temple's men occupied a series of slit trenches near a cut in the riverbank, which allowed vehicles to move into and out of the ford site to Temple's direct front (1). There the fighting patrol waited for the enemy. Around 11.30pm, Temple's men heard splashing and rustling sounds from the north bank. Temple fired several flares to illuminate the crossing site and spotted Chinese soldiers fording the river

in strength. Temple called in artillery while his patrol poured machine-gun and rifle fire into the oncoming Chinese as Temple requested artillery support from every gun that 45 Field Regiment had (2). The Chinese soldiers on the opposite side of the river from Temple's men were the advanced guard of the 187th Division and carried only the bare necessities – clothing, ammunition, food and water (3). The most heavily armed among the Chinese carried their individual weapon – a rifle or 'burp' gun – as well as satchel charges or grenade bandoliers for use against fortified positions or enemy armoured vehicles (4). Tactical communications were also far more rudimentary than the radios available to the British; Chinese company and platoon commanders relied on bugles and gongs (5). The Chinese may have been a low-technology army, but they had the advantage of numbers against Temple's fighting patrol. Despite the accurate, lethal fire that Temple's men poured into the advancing Chinese, Chinese troops managed to cross in numbers and mass on the south bank of the river. At this point, Temple received permission from Carne to withdraw to the Glosters' main positions.

Flares sent up along the Imjin River to illuminate enemy patrols. (IWM)

that linked the forward platoons to the company headquarters, meaning that the Chinese could efficiently prevent 2 and 3 Platoons from receiving ammunition resupply and evacuating their casualties. Nor could the platoons withdraw without being slaughtered. The situation was dire.

To solve this problem, Maj. Pat Angier, the A Company commander, ordered Lt. Phil Curtis of 1 Platoon to assault the Chinese machine gun. By this point it was almost dawn. In the daylight, a direct assault on an entrenched enemy machine gun would be even more dangerous than at night. Curtis organized his men into an assault element – called a 'winkle group' – of five men. The rest of the platoon would provide covering fire. However, as the winkle group approached the bunker, the Chinese troops saw them and turned their fire against Curtis's men. A hail of grenades and gunfire erupted from the Chinese-occupied bunker. The winkle group dived for cover. The attack had faltered. But then Curtis stood, raised his revolver, and charged the bunker by himself. He was shot twice, in the left side and right arm, and collapsed. Wounded but undaunted, Curtis stood up and charged the bunker a second time. Another burst of machine-gun fire struck and killed him, but in the split-second before being hit, he tossed a grenade into the bunker. The explosion killed the Chinese occupants and opened the resupply route for 2 and 3 Platoons. Lieutenant Curtis was posthumously awarded the Victoria Cross.

As Curtis assaulted the bunker, more Chinese massed for another charge up the front slopes towards 2 and 3 Platoons. The Glosters lobbed hand grenades as Maj. Angier called in mortar and artillery fire on the Chinese as they began the attack. Suffering heavy casualties, the Chinese retreated and regrouped at the base of the hill. However, after dawn broke, A Company could no longer hold on. In addition to Curtis, the lieutenant in charge of 2 Platoon and Maj. Angier had both been killed. All surviving officers were wounded, leaving the company sergeant-major in charge.

A view of Hill 148 (left) and D Company's original position (right), as seen from the forward slopes of Hill 235. (Soldiers of Gloucestershire Museum)

Immediately to the east of A Company, D Company's first brush with the Chinese was limited to firing Vickers machine guns at Chinese troops climbing Castle Site. As D Company's machine-gunners fired in support of A Company, Chinese infantry silently infiltrated beyond A Company to the slopes of D Company's position on Hill 182. Chinese bugles and whistles alerted D Company to the danger. Firing flares into the air, D Company's left-flank platoon could see Chinese troops about 35m (40 yards) away. The Glosters immediately opened fire and the surviving Chinese retreated. This attack, however, was only a probe. The main assault came a few minutes later as hundreds of Chinese troops surged forward. Second Lieutenant Denys Whatmore, leading 11 Platoon on the company's left flank, organized the defence, but the Chinese charge was supported by accurate machine-gun fire that killed several of the defending Glosters. Under intense pressure, D Company's acting commander, Capt. Mike Harvey, called for mortar support. But the mortars were low on ammunition. Whatmore's 11 Platoon, meanwhile, was also running out of ammunition. Harvey ordered 11 Platoon to fall back to the company headquarters. They had lost 23 out of 36 men in the platoon.

By dawn on 23 April, the Glosters' A and D Companies were barely hanging on. They would soon be cut off from the rest of the battalion if not withdrawn quickly. B and C Companies, however, had faced little contact during the night. In the centre of 29th Brigade's position, the Royal Northumberland Fusiliers' X and Z Companies had been overrun. Y Company, although it had held its ground, was isolated and in danger of being surrounded. W Company had also been attacked during the night, but held on with little trouble. The Ulsters' battle patrol had been routed, but the rest of the battalion was ready for action, having been held back as the brigade reserve. All Belgian companies had been engaged during the night, but they still held their well-fortified position on Hill 194.

The Chinese offensive had struck the entire I Corps front line. The US 25th Division, with its attached Turkish Brigade, and the US 24th Division both had to retreat from Line Utah. To the east of the 29th Brigade, the remainder of US 3rd Division had stood fast. The ROK 1st Division, covering the hills to the west of the Glosters' A Company, had also held firm through the night. From the Chinese perspective, the attacks against the ROK 1st Division stalled before ever truly beginning. The 64th Army, deployed to the west of 63rd Army, was supposed to break through the ROK division. But the attacking divisions, the 191st and 192nd, had only been in Korea for a few weeks and were not yet ready for the offensive when Peng Dehuai moved the schedule forward from May until April. The 191st and 192nd Divisions did not have the time needed to conduct adequate reconnaissance along the ROK 1st Division's lines, nor did they understand the daily tide rhythms of the Imjin River. As a result, they had difficulty getting into position and crossing the Imjin during the night. Despite running for part of the distance from the rear areas to their staging points, both Chinese divisions arrived too late to fire a preparatory barrage prior to the infantry assault. To make matters worse, the 64th Army's poor knowledge of the tides led to the drowning of several hundred soldiers from the 191st Division's 572nd Regiment when, between 1.00am and 2.00am, the tide came in and the depth of the river suddenly swelled an additional 4.5m (15ft). Exhausted and disoriented, the 64th Army failed to muster its full strength to attack the ROK troops on the south bank of the Imjin.

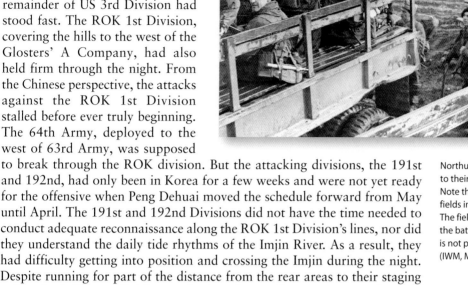

Northumberland Fusiliers move to their front-line positions. Note the ubiquitous rice paddy fields in the background. The fields were dry during the battle, as the rice crop is not planted until May. (IWM, MH 33047)

DAY 2: MONDAY, 23 APRIL

Surveying the situation, Brig. Brodie could see that this was no small probing attack. The Chinese had shattered the centre of his position and had done significant damage to the Glosters on the brigade's left flank. At 9.00am on 23 April, Eighth Army commander Lt. Gen. Van Fleet ordered a general withdrawal from Line Utah to Line Kansas. This decision meant that 29th Brigade had to hold its position, which would allow US 3rd Division to fall back safely without exposing its flank to Chinese attack. Brodie knew that his most important task was to protect Route 33, which was 3rd Division's primary route of retreat. In order to keep 3rd Division protected, however, Brodie had to leave the Belgians in place for as long as possible. But if he left the Belgians in their current position for too long, they would be encircled and overrun. Furthermore, the Glosters were in trouble on the brigade's left flank. Before the battle began, the Glosters were already the most isolated of Brodie's battalions, because they were separated from the rest of the brigade by the mountain of Kamaksan. But Brodie's most

pressing concern was to protect his centre. If the centre broke, the Glosters and Belgians would both be surrounded and the Chinese could rush down Route 11 and seize the intersection between Route 11 and Route 33. Such a move would split the UN lines in two and allow the Chinese to turn east and crush the US 3rd Division or turn west and annihilate the ROK 1st Division. Either way, if the Chinese destroyed 3rd Division, I Corps would be broken in two and the road to Uijeongbu – and hence the gateway to Seoul – would be open.

29th Brigade Consolidates

To shore up the centre of his position, Brodie decided to commit the Royal Ulster Rifles, deploying all but B Company to Hill 398. Located behind the Fusiliers' positions, Hill 398 dominated the approaches to Route 11 and the valley below. It was a strong position. B Company, meanwhile, remained about 6km (4 miles) to the south, where there was a chokepoint near Hwangbang-ni – a pass in which Route 11 crossed over a saddle between two hills. Brodie also knew that, with daylight, he would be able to call upon the Centurion tanks of C Squadron, 8th Hussars and close air support from the F-80 'Shooting Star' fighter-bombers of the US 5th Air Force.

Brodie next had to decide what to do about his flanks. Of the Belgian and Gloster predicaments, the Belgians' was more pressing at the moment. At around 7.30am, Brodie contacted the US 3rd Division commander, Maj. Gen. Soule, who told Brodie that he would receive air cover as well as a US infantry company reinforced with two tank platoons to support the Belgians. Soule also promised to commit 1st Battalion, 7th US Infantry (1/7th Infantry), which was part of his division reserve, to the 29th Brigade. Having secured support from his higher headquarters, Brodie next turned to dealing with the Glosters' situation. Shortly before 8.00am, he radioed Lt. Col. Carne and gave him permission to withdraw A and D Companies.

Withdrawing A and D Companies was more complicated than it appeared. Both units were in close combat with the enemy. They would have to leave their defensive positions, exposing themselves to enemy fire in the process,

and then move down the hill as Chinese troops occupied the top of the hill and fired from the crest at the retreating Glosters. Aerial reconnaissance reported nearly a thousand Chinese troops preparing to assault the positions. Carne decided to pull each company back one at a time, with A Company the first to go. With fewer than 60 soldiers still fighting, the survivors of A Company retreated while D Company provided covering fire. An airstrike obliterated the first Chinese elements to reach the slit trenches that A Company had vacated minutes earlier. Once the A Company survivors reached the valley floor, they rendezvoused with the battalion's remaining Oxford carriers and moved towards the battalion headquarters on Hill 235. With A Company temporarily out of danger, D Company began its withdrawal. Under cover from mortar fire and a short but effective barrage from all of 45 Field Regiment's guns, D Company broke contact and retreated towards Hill 235. Whether because of the bombardment or exhaustion, the Chinese decided not to pursue the Glosters.

Carne's dispositions now included the battered remnants of A and D Companies, as well as his Support Company, on Hill 235. Soon to become known as Gloster Hill, Hill 235 lay on the west side of Route 5Y just above the tiny hamlet of Seolma-ri. C Company held the high ground directly to their front. Carne also ordered B Company to redeploy on Hill 316, a high point several hundred metres east of C Company on the same ridgeline. B Company had to clear the hill of a small Chinese force, but the Glosters had occupied it by 10.45am. The entire battalion was now deployed tightly around the high ground controlling Route 5Y. As the Glosters dug in, Chinese follow-on forces pushed past the Glosters and around their flanks, seeking to encircle the battalion and isolate them from the rest of 29th Brigade. The Glosters soon realized this when, on a mission to brigade headquarters, battalion second-in-command Maj. Digby Grist's jeep drove past the battalion's Forward Echelon supply depot, 8km (5 miles) south along Route 5Y, only to discover that the Chinese had captured it. Miraculously, Grist and his driver swerved through a hail of Chinese gunfire without being harmed and safely reached the brigade command post.

29TH BRIGADE'S EASTERN DEFENCES, 23 APRIL 1951

29th Brigade consolidates and reorganizes along Route 11: approximately 5.00am to 8.00pm, 23 April 1951

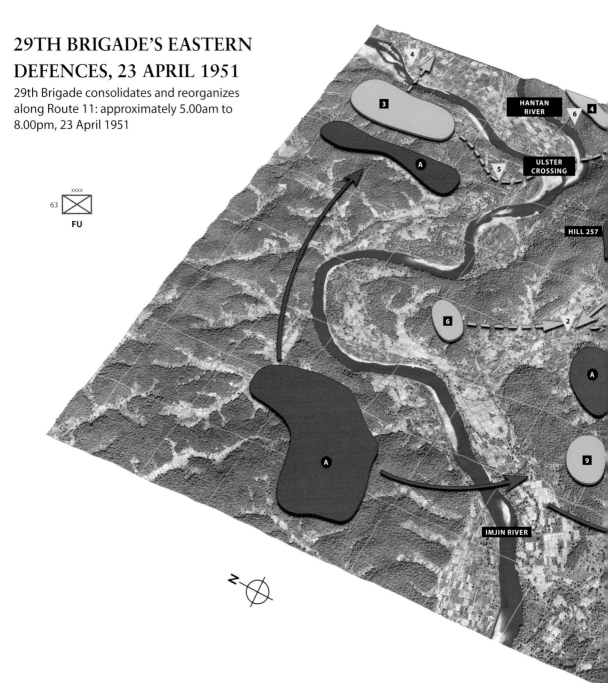

EVENTS

1. During the night of 22–23 April, Brig. Brodie commits his reserve, the Royal Ulster Rifles, to secure Hill 398. He orders the Rifles' B Company to remain in place at the 'saddle' near Hwangbang-ni.

2. After daybreak, Brodie despatches C Squadron, 8th King's Royal Irish Hussars to extricate Y Company, Royal Northumberland Fusiliers from their isolated position along the Imjin. With the Hussars' Centurion tanks and additional support from airstrikes on Chinese positions, Y Company safely returns to British lines. The operation is complete by early afternoon. W Company and X Company also withdraw, taking position along the ridgeline that parallels Route 11 to the west.

3. Brodie orders Z Company, Royal Northumberland Fusiliers, to launch a counter-attack against Hill 257. Around 1.00pm, the attack commences. Airstrikes and artillery bombard Chinese positions on the hilltop, but the attacking Z Company infantrymen make little headway. After 20 minutes, the Fusilier battalion commander, Lt. Col.

Foster, calls off the attack. Z Company later repositions to the south of X Company, north-west of the 29th Brigade headquarters.

4. By 6.00pm, the situation to 29th Brigade's right flank stabilized to the point where Brodie could now withdraw the Belgian Battalion on Hill 194 without exposing other 3rd Infantry Division units to flank attacks. Dismounted infantrymen ford the Imjin River to the east.

5. In a mad dash, the battalion's vehicles convoy across the Ulster Crossing pontoon bridges.

6. The Belgians' retreat is supported by UN aircraft and a feint by the 1st Battalion, 7th US Infantry Regiment. These efforts keep the Chinese pinned down while the Belgians fall back. By 8.00pm, the Belgians begin to regroup along Route 33, further to the east.

7. Chinese forces from the 187th Division continue to advance south along the river. Many of these troops head for the slopes of Kamaksan, thereby slicing 29th Brigade in two – the Glosters to the west along Route 5Y, and the remainder of 29th Brigade to the east along Route 11.

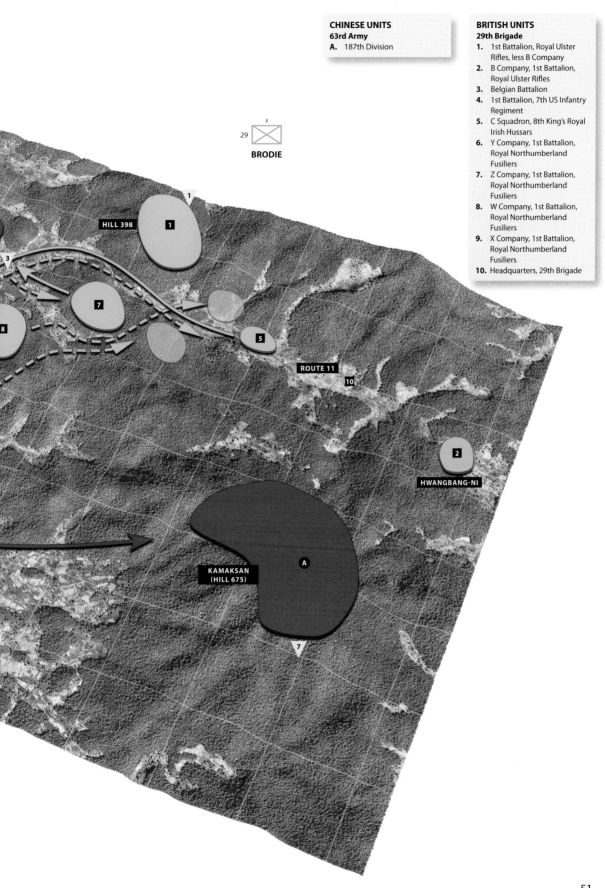

CHINESE UNITS
63rd Army
A. 187th Division

BRITISH UNITS
29th Brigade
1. 1st Battalion, Royal Ulster Rifles, less B Company
2. B Company, 1st Battalion, Royal Ulster Rifles
3. Belgian Battalion
4. 1st Battalion, 7th US Infantry Regiment
5. C Squadron, 8th King's Royal Irish Hussars
6. Y Company, 1st Battalion, Royal Northumberland Fusiliers
7. Z Company, 1st Battalion, Royal Northumberland Fusiliers
8. W Company, 1st Battalion, Royal Northumberland Fusiliers
9. X Company, 1st Battalion, Royal Northumberland Fusiliers
10. Headquarters, 29th Brigade

29 X

BRODIE

HILL 398

ROUTE 11

HWANGBANG-NI

KAMAKSAN
(HILL 675)

Throughout its ordeal, 29th Brigade could rely on fighter-bombers such as these F-80 Shooting Stars for close air support. (© CORBIS/Corbis via Getty Images)

In the Northumberlands' position, Y Company had not been attacked during the night, but now found themselves surrounded by Chinese forces who had isolated them from the rest of the brigade. Brodie needed to pull Y Company back from their current, exposed, position and unite them with the rest of their battalion. To do so, he would have to punch a hole in the Chinese lines so that the trapped Fusiliers could escape. Brodie ordered the Centurion tanks of C Squadron, 8th King's Royal Irish Hussars to move up the valley, break through the Chinese lines and extricate Y Company. As the Centurions rolled forwards, F-80 fighter-bombers dropped napalm on Chinese troop concentrations behind Y Company. The bombing runs effectively cleared the way for the Centurions, who arrived in the vicinity of Y Company without heavy contact with the enemy. By early afternoon, Y Company had been extricated.

After Y Company and the Hussars rumbled back to friendly lines, Lt. Col. Foster ordered Z Company to counter-attack to recapture Hill 257, which they had lost during the previous night. Hill 257 overlooked the Belgian position on Hill 194; retaking it would help open an escape route for the beleaguered Belgians. Around 1.00pm, Foster called for several airstrikes on the Chinese occupying the hill as well as fire support from the Hussars' Centurions before sending Z Company forwards. The attack quickly faltered. During a brisk 20-minute fight, the Fusiliers nearly reached the crest of the hill only to be thrown back by a resolute Chinese defence that involved a volley of hand grenades and a human wave counter-attack. However, before Foster could prepare another attack, Brodie arrived at the Fusiliers' headquarters. He ordered Foster to move the battalion further south along Route 11, in between the road and the Ulsters' positions on Hill 398. The redeployment was complete by 3.00pm.

As the Glosters came under increasing pressure from Chinese assaults, Lt. Col. Carne decided to consolidate his battalion on the forbidding summit of Hill 235, which dominated the terrain around it. (Soldiers of Gloucestershire Museum)

As the Fusiliers repositioned, so did the 65th US Infantry Regiment, on 29th Brigade's right flank. On the morning of 23 April, the Turkish Brigade – on the right flank of the 65th Infantry – had to retreat. The Turks had put up a strong defence against tremendous odds, even fighting hand-to-hand through the night, but had suffered heavy casualties and were ordered to fall back south of the Hantan River. This withdrawal exposed the 65th Infantry's right flank, so they too had to fall back. The 65th Infantry's left flank, however, was still anchored on the Belgian battalion. The Belgians therefore had to hold Hill 194 until the 65th Infantry could withdraw. By 1.30pm, the 65th had successfully withdrawn to a rear staging area at the intersection of Route 11 and Route 33. Meanwhile, 1/7th Infantry – the reinforcements that Maj. Gen. Soule had promised earlier in the day – arrived to help extricate the Belgians.

A view of Hill 235, across the valley floor, as the Chinese would have seen it after occupying A Company's position on Hill 148. This picture was taken five weeks after the battle. (IWM, BF 10277)

The Withdrawal from Hill 194

With 65th Infantry having successfully relocated, Brodie could now withdraw the Belgians. The plan was for 1/7th Infantry to assault Hill 257 as a diversion, while two platoons of US Army Sherman tanks and a company of infantry secured the pontoon bridges at Ulster Crossing. Belgian vehicles would drive across the bridges to safety while the infantry forded the Hantan River. On Hill 194, Lt. Col. Crahay ordered 2nd Lt. Henri Wolfs the job of rear-guard. Leading an infantry squad and two machine-gun-armed jeeps, Wolfs was to keep the Chinese at bay long enough for the rest of the battalion to escape.

The operation began at 6.00pm. American artillery and airstrikes kept the Chinese pinned down as 1/7th Infantry assaulted Hill 257, meeting little resistance in the process. American tanks thundered towards Ulster Crossing and opened fire to suppress Chinese positions on the opposite bank. Better against infantry than British Centurions because of their coaxial and turret-mounted machine guns, the Shermans quickly dispersed any Chinese who were still in the open on the north bank of the river. The Belgians' vehicle-borne element drove out first, firing wildly behind them as they sped across the bridges. The enemy, however, was suffering from the artillery and air barrage and could only respond with light, harassing fire. Next, the Belgian infantry waded into the river. The water levels were low enough that the river proved easily fordable. As the Belgians evacuated Hill 194, some Chinese troops decided to follow behind and occupy the now-vacant trenches. It proved a fatal decision, as American aircraft incinerated the Chinese with napalm dropped on the old Belgian positions. Under a protective curtain of artillery and airstrikes, Lt. Wolfs and his rear-guard were the last to drive across the bridges. By 8.00pm, what remained of the Belgian battalion had successfully escaped.

Reinforcements from 3rd Division had helped extricate the Belgians. Next, Brodie intended to use another unit that Maj. Gen. Soule had given him – the 10th (Philippine) Battalion Combat Team (BCT) – to rescue the Glosters. The Filipino troops had been involved in fierce fighting elsewhere in 3rd Division's sector during the night of 22 April, so they did not arrive in 29th Brigade's area of operations until late afternoon. With darkness approaching, Brodie worried that if he launched a night attack, he would be exposing the Philippine troops to a Chinese ambush. He decided that the best option was to wait until morning. Brodie had been able to send extra ammunition and supplies to the Glosters before the Chinese captured A Echelon, so he believed that Carne's men could hold on through the night. Brodie also arranged for supplies to be airdropped to the Glosters on the morning of Tuesday, 24 April. The next day would prove crucial to determining the Glosters' fate – and that of 29th Brigade.

The Glosters Retreat to Hill 235
Throughout the night of 23–24 April, B and C Companies bore the brunt of the Chinese assaults. Around 11.00pm, the attack began. It started with small probing attacks to identify the locations of British strengths such as machine-gun positions, booby traps and kill zones, as well as any gaps in B Company's defences. Next came a brief mortar barrage on B Company's positions, followed by the bugle calls that sounded the beginning of the main assault. The Chinese advanced in a human wave, which the Glosters met with a hail of gunfire. As one wave would stall, the Chinese troops would fall back, regroup and launch another assault. The fighting went on for about an hour, with hundreds of casualties for the Chinese. But B Company also took heavy casualties. When Chinese attackers closed within 18m (20 yards) of British slit trenches, a hail of grenades and burp gun blasts followed.

In the darkness, both sides were largely shooting at the other side's muzzle flashes. With B Company occupying static defences, Chinese troops could easily pinpoint muzzle flashes from the Glosters' positions and concentrate machine-gun and mortar fire on them to cover the advancing infantrymen. As Chinese machine guns raked B Company's trenches, British artillery rained down on the attackers. B Company's forward observer alternated his calls for fire support by first targeting the attacking infantry, then shifting to the Chinese mortars and machine guns, before shifting fire back to the infantry. Some of the barrages came as close as 45m (50 yards) from the Glosters' positions. This cycle continued until 45 Field Regiment's howitzers had to pause for fear of overheating from constant firing. Airbursts added to the devastating effects of artillery and mortar fire. Many shells fired by both

sides exploded in the trees above ground level, sending wooden shards flying in all directions and causing additional wounds and sometimes fatal injuries.

As B Company defended Hill 316, C Company – deployed to B Company's left – also came under attack. Unlike the advance warning that B Company's reconnaissance patrol provided, C Company was taken by surprise. The company headquarters and 7 Platoon held their ground, but the 8 and 9 Platoon positions were overrun. Carne ordered C Company to retreat to Hill 235. With C Company retreating and B Company barely hanging on, Carne ordered the battalion headquarters and Support Company up Hill 235 to join D and A Companies. C Troop of the 170 Mortar Battery, unable to carry their mortar tubes up the hill, destroyed the equipment so that it would not fall into Chinese hands before joining the Glosters on Hill 235. C Troop fought alongside the Glosters as infantrymen for the rest of the battle. Carne had managed to consolidate much of his surviving force on a strong defensive position, but B Company's position remained precarious. In total, he had consolidated 400 unwounded men from his battalion on Hill 235. Many of the wounded had been evacuated to the brigade rear area before A Echelon had been captured but, having been surrounded, Carne's battalion medical staff now had to care for the remaining casualties on their own. Furthermore, based on what his men could see of Chinese movements around them, Carne estimated that a Chinese regiment had infiltrated between Hill 235 and the rest of 29th Brigade. Even so, Carne and his men had reason to be hopeful: they heard the news that the Philippine 10th BCT reinforcements had arrived in the brigade area.

From the Chinese vantage point, the situation offered a mixture of frustration and encouragement. As the 63rd Army hammered at the British 29th Brigade, to the west, 64th Army's attack remained stalled. By the afternoon of 23 April, Nineteenth Army Group commander Yang Dezhi knew he needed to revitalize the 64th Army attack if he hoped to achieve the breakout towards Uijeongbu that his plan called for. Yang therefore ordered the 64th Army to crush the ROK 1st Division, on the Glosters' left flank. To emphasize the importance that he placed on breaking through, Yang informed 64th Army commander Zeng Siyu that failure would result

THE ASSAULT ON THE GLOSTERS

The Chinese assault on the Glosters' positions: 10.30pm,
22 April to approximately 10.00am, 24 April 1951

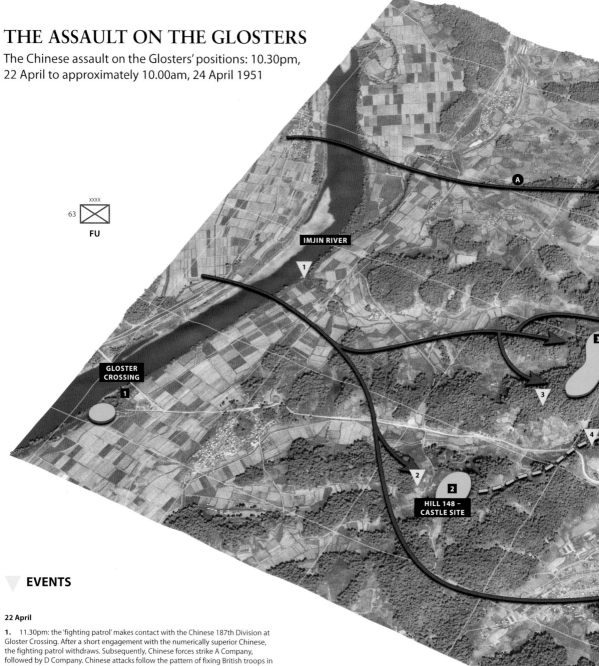

EVENTS

22 April

1. 11.30pm: the 'fighting patrol' makes contact with the Chinese 187th Division at Gloster Crossing. After a short engagement with the numerically superior Chinese, the fighting patrol withdraws. Subsequently, Chinese forces strike A Company, followed by D Company. Chinese attacks follow the pattern of fixing British troops in their hilltop positions while sending follow-on forces around the flanks of the British positions to infiltrate further into the British defensive zone.

2. 12.00am: 187th Division penetrates A Company's perimeter. Lieutenant Phil Curtis leads a successful counter-attack, but is killed in the process. He will later receive the Victoria Cross for his gallantry.

23 April

3. 7.50am: air reconnaissance reports thousands of Chinese troops attacking A and D Companies, with Chinese reinforcements outflanking the two forward companies. Lieutenant-Colonel Carne requests permission from Brig. Brodie to withdraw A and D Companies to Hill 235.

4. 8.00am: having received permission from Brodie, Carne orders A/1 GLOS to retreat to Hill 235 under covering fire from D Company.

5. 8.30am: once A Company has withdrawn safely, D Company falls back.

6. 10.45am: having encountered only sporadic contact through the night, B Company had not suffered any casualties. But with D Company withdrawing, B Company's flank was exposed. B Company withdraws to Hill 316, only to discover that the Chinese had already occupied it. B Company drives the Chinese off the hill with a bayonet charge.

7. In the early afternoon, Maj. Digby Grist from A Echelon (the Glosters' Support Company) brings supplies to battalion headquarters. Around this time, A Echelon (deployed off the map's southern boundary) was overrun. The Glosters are now surrounded.

8. 11.00pm: the Chinese 189th Division arrives on the battlefield in the vicinity of Kamaksan. The 189th launches several attacks against B Company throughout the night.

24 April

9. 3.30am: 189th Division breaks through the C Company perimeter and begin infiltrating between B and C Companies. About half an hour later, Carne orders the battalion HQ and support elements up to Hill 235.

10. Sometime between 5.00am and 8.00am: Confusion in the C Company lines results in the unit's withdrawal. B Company is now in danger of being isolated.

11. Shortly after 8.00am, the Chinese overrun B Company; of the 120 soldiers who began the battle with B Company, only about 20 escape to Hill 235.

12. By 10.00am, Lt. Col. Carne has consolidated the remnants of his battalion on Hill 235. The Glosters would hold these positions for another 24 hours.

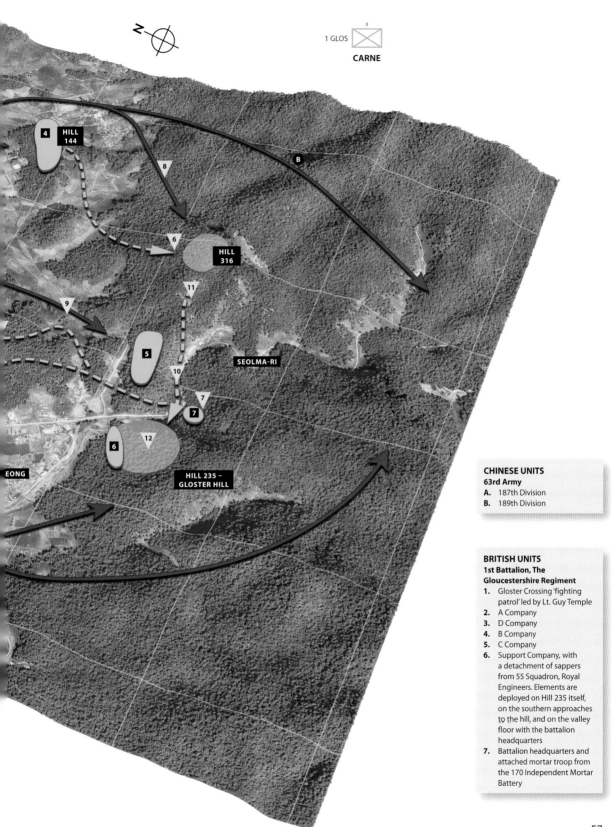

1 GLOS ⊠
CARNE

N

HILL 144

HILL 316

SEOLMA-RI

EONG

HILL 235 – GLOSTER HILL

CHINESE UNITS
63rd Army
A. 187th Division
B. 189th Division

BRITISH UNITS
1st Battalion, The Gloucestershire Regiment
1. Gloster Crossing 'fighting patrol' led by Lt. Guy Temple
2. A Company
3. D Company
4. B Company
5. C Company
6. Support Company, with a detachment of sappers from 55 Squadron, Royal Engineers. Elements are deployed on Hill 235 itself, on the southern approaches to the hill, and on the valley floor with the battalion headquarters
7. Battalion headquarters and attached mortar troop from the 170 Independent Mortar Battery

Soldiers from the US 65th Infantry Regiment, to the right flank of 29th Brigade, take cover from Chinese small-arms fire. Recruited from Puerto Rico, the 65th was a battle-hardened regiment famous for its 31 January 1951 bayonet charge that resulted in the capture of a strategically vital hill south of Seoul. (Bettmann/Getty Images)

in 'severe punishment by our revolutionary disciplines' and that 'any unsuccessful attack means death'. Fully comprehending the implications, Zeng committed his reserve division, the 190th. The attack was ready to commence shortly before dawn. Heartened by the renewed push that 64th Army was preparing to launch, Yang was also encouraged by the news that by 4.00am on 24 April, the 63rd Army had completely surrounded the Glosters. In order to seize Uijeongbu and split the UN forces north of Seoul, the Chinese needed a quick breakthrough in one of two sectors: that of ROK 1st Division or the Glosters.

DAY 3: TUESDAY, 24 APRIL

In the early morning hours of 24 April and to the east of the Glosters, both the Royal Northumberland Fusiliers and the Royal Ulster Rifles faced a series of assaults. Beginning around 2.15am east of Route 11 on Hill 398, the Royal Ulster Rifles held off several human wave attacks. In a manner similar to the attacks against the Glosters' B Company, Chinese troops advanced to the sound of bugles, with human waves rushing the British positions as machine guns and mortars provided supporting fire for the attacking infantry. In one instance, Chinese soldiers, unable to gain further ground in the assault, took cover behind a pile of rocks in front of the Ulsters' A Company. Seeing the Chinese trying to dig in, A Company let loose a volley of bazooka fire that had the effect of an artillery barrage. The fighting continued until dawn, when UN aircraft came to the Ulsters' aid. The subsequent airstrikes disrupted Chinese staging areas at the base of Hill 398. During many of these sorties, UN fighter-bombers dropped napalm to devastating effect, incinerating many Chinese and generating the sickening smell of burned flesh. Despite the bombing, Chinese troops pressed their attacks with limited infantry assaults supported by machine-gun fire.

Meanwhile, at around 3.15am, the Northumberland Fusiliers' positions west of Route 11 also came under attack. Although W Company held its position, Y Company retreated to the valley floor. Chinese soldiers poured into Y Company's recently abandoned position, but after daybreak, Lt. Col. Foster sent X Company along with several of the Hussars' Centurion tanks to plug the gap. With the advantages of daylight and the Centurions' 20-pounder main guns, W Company kept the Chinese pinned down.

As Brig. Brodie surveyed the scene on the morning of 24 April, he knew that he would have to launch a rescue attempt for the Glosters. He had 10th Philippine BCT and the Centurions of C Squadron, 8th Hussars available, but at 7.00am Lt. Col. Carne radioed the Brigade headquarters with an alternative suggestion. Carne recommended that the Glosters attempt a breakout to the south. However, such a limited withdrawal ran contrary to Eighth Army commander Lt. Gen. Van Fleet's instructions. Van Fleet had ordered all UN forces to withdraw to Line Kansas, but fearing the potential of a disorganized retreat like that which had occurred in November 1950 with the initial Chinese intervention in the war, he decided to hold Line Kansas for as long as possible. When Brodie informed Maj. Gen. Soule of Carne's request, permission for the breakout was denied due to Van Fleet's instructions to hold Line Kansas. The Glosters were not to withdraw further for the time being. Soule did, however, encourage Brodie to send the 10th BCT forward in support of the Glosters.

Failure to Relieve the Glosters

At 8.00am, 29th Brigade initiated the relief attempt. The relief force consisted of Filipino infantry from 10th BCT, four Filipino M-24 Chaffee light tanks and a troop of Centurions from the Hussars. The Hussars were encouraged by the return of their commander, Maj. Henry Huth, who had rushed back from leave in Japan when the battle began. He would lead the armoured element, while the Glosters' second-in-command, Maj. Grist, who had escaped from A Echelon the previous day, and Philippine Lt. Col. Dionisio Ojeda led the overall effort.

The relief column would have to travel north along Route 5Y to rendezvous with the Glosters. It was about 7km (4½ miles) from the staging area in the Brigade rear to the Glosters' position on Hill 235. Route 5Y was a narrow dirt road, but about 4km (2½ miles) south of Hill 235 the road entered a gorge with steep, tight defiles on either side. As a result, the plan was for the Filipino infantry to advance along the hills on both sides of 5Y to clear Chinese infantry, while the Chaffee and Centurion tanks moved along the road. This way, the tanks could provide fire support for the infantry while the infantry simultaneously covered the flanks of the tank column from Chinese ambush. Evidently, a route reconnaissance had not been performed on 5Y prior to the battle to determine whether Centurions could fit through the defiles. Because the Hussars did not know whether their tanks could fit through the gorge, it was decided that the Chaffees would lead the armoured thrust. Much smaller than the bulky Centurions, the Chaffees could manoeuvre more easily along the narrow road. The Centurions would follow behind so as not to block the progress of the rest of the column if the road narrowed to such an extent that they could no longer pass through. This decision was logical in terms

29th Brigade Defence of Route 11, 24 April

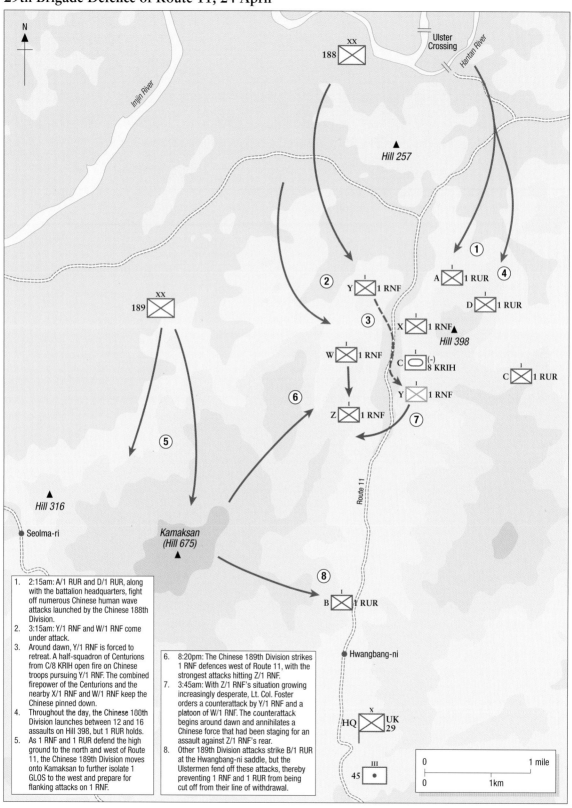

N

Imjin River

Ulster Crossing

Hantan River

188 | XX

Hill 257

① ④

189 | XX

② Y | 1 RNF

A | 1 RUR

D | 1 RUR

③

X | 1 RNF ▲
Hill 398

W | 1 RNF

C | (-) 8 KRIH

C | 1 RUR

⑥

Z | 1 RNF

Y | 1 RNF

⑦

⑤

Hill 316

Kamaksan
(Hill 675) ▲

Seolma-ri

⑧

Route 11

B | 1 RUR

Hwangbang-ni

HQ | X UK 29

45 | III •

1. 2:15am: A/1 RUR and D/1 RUR, along with the battalion headquarters, fight off numerous Chinese human wave attacks launched by the Chinese 188th Division.
2. 3:15am: Y/1 RNF and W/1 RNF come under attack.
3. Around dawn, Y/1 RNF is forced to retreat. A half-squadron of Centurions from C/8 KRIH open fire on Chinese troops pursuing Y/1 RNF. The combined firepower of the Centurions and the nearby X/1 RNF and W/1 RNF keep the Chinese pinned down.
4. Throughout the day, the Chinese 100th Division launches between 12 and 16 assaults on Hill 398, but 1 RUR holds.
5. As 1 RNF and 1 RUR defend the high ground to the north and west of Route 11, the Chinese 189th Division moves onto Kamaksan to further isolate 1 GLOS to the west and prepare for flanking attacks on 1 RNF.

6. 8:20pm: The Chinese 189th Division strikes 1 RNF defences west of Route 11, with the strongest attacks hitting Z/1 RNF.
7. 3:45am: With Z/1 RNF's situation growing increasingly desperate, Lt. Col. Foster orders a counterattack by Y/1 RNF and a platoon of W/1 RNF. The counterattack begins around dawn and annihilates a Chinese force that had been staging for an assault against Z/1 RNF's rear.
8. Other 189th Division attacks strike B/1 RUR at the Hwangbang-ni saddle, but the Ulstermen fend off these attacks, thereby preventing 1 RNF and 1 RUR from being cut off from their line of withdrawal.

0 | 1 mile
0 | 1km

of mobility, but it had the effect of placing the lightly armoured tanks in the front, where they were more vulnerable to anti-tank fire.

By 9.00am, the relief force had recaptured the Glosters' A Echelon position and entered the gorge on 5Y. Quick progress slowed as the Filipino infantry had to crawl along the rocky slopes of the hills on either side of the gorge. The relief column thus far had made little contact with the enemy. Over the next few hours, the column encountered sporadic small-arms and mortar fire, but continued to roll slowly forwards. By 2.15pm, the relief force was about 2.5km (1½ miles) away from the Glosters.

This Filipino M24 Chaffee light tank blocked Route 5Y when it was disabled, which prevented the relief effort from reaching the Glosters. It is shown here several weeks later, after it had been bulldozed off the road. (Soldiers of Gloucestershire Museum)

As luck would have it, the terrain began to open up as well. The column reached a point along 5Y where the gorge widened, allowing vehicles to manoeuvre in a small open space a few hundred metres wide consisting of several rice paddies and a few farmers' homes.

This was precisely the location where the Chinese had planned their ambush. Just as it exited the defile and entered the open ground, the lead Filipino Chaffee tank struck an anti-tank mine, exploded and caught fire. Above the defile, the forested ridgelines erupted with rifle and machine-gun fire. Two battalions of Chinese infantry – one from the 561st Regiment of 187th Division and one from the 564th Regiment of 188th Division – had dug in along the ridges overlooking both sides of the road. The advancing Filipino infantry, many of whom had descended from the ridges as the ground flattened near the rice paddies, dived for cover wherever they could find it. Some jumped into drainage ditches, others were mowed down by the Chinese. Another Chaffee tried to push the burning hulk of the lead tank off the road, but to no avail. Behind the Chaffees, the Hussars' Centurions were too big to drive around the disabled Filipino tank on such a narrow road. The Centurions also lacked pintle-mounted machine guns, so they could not fire at the Chinese positions at the top of the steep slopes around them. To make matters worse, Chinese anti-tank troops armed with pole charges and sticky bombs were preparing to assault the stalled tanks. Sensing the danger, Maj. Huth ordered the armoured column to pull back.

Taken by surprise, the relief force called for air support. Aircraft soon appeared overhead and attacked the Chinese positions. In between bombing runs, the Filipino infantry launched several assaults against the Chinese, but without result. The paddy fields meant that any attack to the front would expose the infantry to a murderous crossfire, but any attempt to move around the open ground required assaulting Chinese troops holding the high ground around the clearing. There was little that the Filipino and British tanks could do at this point, too, as they could not move forward past the destroyed Chaffee. By 4.15pm, the relief effort had stalled. At 5.30pm, after two hours of fighting, the relief column withdrew.

There is some uncertainty and controversy over whether senior leaders from 3rd Division, I Corps and Eighth Army properly understood the seriousness of the Glosters' situation. According to the British Army's official history of the conflict, written by former Gloster adjutant Anthony Farrar-Hockley, there was a miscommunication between Brodie and Maj. Gen. Soule. As the 10th BCT and Hussar relief column snaked its way along Route 5Y during the afternoon, Soule informed Brodie that he was preparing a second relief force from 3rd Division comprised of two battalions from the 65th US Infantry Regiment, the 64th Tank Battalion and an additional artillery battalion. Soule's plan was to stage this second relief force in 29th Brigade's rear area between Route 11 and Route 33. Early on the morning of 25 April, the 65th Infantry and its supporting armoured and artillery units would drive west towards Hill 424, filling the gap between the Glosters and the Northumberlands, thus stabilizing the entire 29th Brigade line.

As he explained the plan to Brodie, Soule asked 'How are the Glosters doing?' Brodie replied 'A bit sticky; things are pretty sticky down there.' Farrar-Hockley believed that Soule interpreted this characteristic British understatement as an 'unpleasant but sustainable' situation, when in fact the Glosters were in dire straits. Soule ordered the Glosters to hold their position in expectation of launching another relief attempt the following day. When Brodie informed Carne of the instructions, Carne replied by saying 'I understand the position quite clearly. What I must make clear to you is that my command is no longer an effective fighting force. If it is required that we shall stay here, in spite of this, we shall continue to hold.'[1]

Some scholars of the battle have asserted that had Brodie described the situation more clearly, Soule might have committed reinforcements sooner, which could have rescued the Glosters from their plight. However, this interpretation overestimates the availability of reinforcements and the speed with which they could have been committed to the Glosters' relief. UN forces were heavily pressed across the entire line, and the 65th US Infantry had been engaged in bitter fighting since the Chinese offensive began. The 65th Infantry had only recently been pulled off the line and only for the purpose of reinforcing the British, nor were they available to support 29th Brigade until the evening of 24 April. This meant that, at the earliest, the 65th Infantry might have been able to launch a night attack. But attacking in the darkness across the rear of allied units against an enemy known for its ability to manoeuvre at night was a recipe for disaster. Brodie's understatement notwithstanding, the morning of 25 April was the earliest that a second relief effort could reasonably begin.

The strength of Chinese forces was also a consideration when planning for the Glosters' relief. In the official history, Farrar-Hockley assessed that, given the size of the Chinese force holding the clearing on 5Y, 'a reinforced brigade or a regimental combat team was the minimum force required to affect a relief'.[2] This was true, given what Carne, Farrar-Hockley and other senior UN commanders believed about the strength of the Chinese defences along Route 5Y. There was no way for them to know that UN air strikes had actually devastated the Chinese defenders to such an extent that the first relief force from 10th BCT and the Hussars had almost succeeded. On the Chinese side, the 561st Regiment's 5th and 6th Companies had been virtually

1   As quoted in Anthony Farrar-Hockley, *The British Part in the Korean War*. Volume II (London: HMSO, 1995), 127–28.
2   Farrar-Hockley, 127.

C-119 Flying Boxcar aircraft dropped supplies to the Glosters during the battle; however, due to enemy fire and the close proximity of Chinese ground troops to Gloster positions, most supply drops were unsuccessful. (© CORBIS/ Corbis via Getty Images)

wiped out – by evening there were only a handful of survivors. Only one soldier from the 564th Regiment's 7th Company, part of the battalion dug in on the opposite side of Route 5Y, was still combat effective at the end of the day. Altogether, over half of the Chinese defenders had been killed. The Chinese managed to fend off the first relief attempt, but did so only by the slimmest of margins.

While Brodie searched for a way to rescue them, the Glosters had plenty of other immediate problems. During the night of 23–24 April, Carne had managed to consolidate A, C, D and Support Companies along with the battalion headquarters and the mortar troop on Hill 235, but he still had to find a way to extricate B Company from the ridge on the east side of Route 5Y. However, B Company had reached breaking point. Low on ammunition and with so many wounded that they were lying in the company headquarters with little cover from enemy fire, B Company commander Maj. Denis Harding withdrew his platoons into a tighter perimeter to reorganize. Shortly after 8.00am, the Chinese launched their seventh attack. They concentrated their assault on 4 Platoon's positions. Outnumbering the defenders by a significant margin, the Chinese were simply able to overrun 4 Platoon by weight of numbers.

B Company retreated with every man fending for himself. Small groups of soldiers scrambled down the hill and slipped into the woods in an effort to evade capture by the Chinese. A party of about 15 men, led by Maj. Harding, emerged on the hillside across the valley from the battalion positions on Hill 235. Spotting the fleeing B Company men, Glosters on Hill 235 laid down covering fire with Vickers machine guns and Bren guns as the Chinese pursued Harding's group. Under this protective hail of bullets, Harding's B Company remnants descended the hillside, crossed the valley floor and Route 5Y, then climbed to the crest of Hill 235. After a 40-minute trek,

Harding's men were safe, but B Company was no longer an effective fighting force. Carne combined these B Company survivors with the remnants of C Company to form a composite element and assigned them to the south-west sector of the perimeter.

The covering fire for B Company's withdrawal, however, drove the Chinese off the crests of the ridgeline opposite Hill 235. The Glosters spotted an opportunity. On the valley floor at the base of Hill 235, in the area occupied by the mortars and battalion headquarters prior to the battle, stockpiles of ammunition, radio batteries, food, water and medical supplies remained intact and available for use – if the Glosters could reach them. If the Glosters were unable to obtain supplies, they would not be able to hold on much longer. An airdrop of supplies had been planned for earlier in the day, but had been cancelled. But with the Chinese now temporarily pinned down, Regimental Sergeant Major Jack Hobbs quickly led a patrol of Glosters and Korean porters to the old battalion headquarters area to scrounge up as many supplies as possible. As the patrol rushed down the hill, Gloster machine-gunners fired on the opposite ridgelines and the slopes of Kamaksan, while forward observers called on 45 Field Regiment to fire smoke shells to obscure the patrol's movement. The patrol was a success, returning with some food and water, but, most importantly, a large amount of ammunition. Later in the day, second-in-command Maj. Digby Grist, stuck at brigade headquarters since his wild ride through the Chinese-occupied A Echelon position on 23 April, coordinated five airdrops to resupply the beleaguered Glosters, but all except one of the drops failed to land inside the Glosters' perimeter. The one successful drop provided much-needed medical supplies and additional ammunition. Despite the increasingly desperate situation, the Glosters remained committed to the task at hand. That night, as Lt. Col. Carne reorganized his defences to cover the highest ground with the best protection and fields of fire, one soldier assured him that 'we shall be all right, sir, 'twill be like the Rock of Gibraltar up there'.[3]

The Defence of Route 11

While the Glosters fought for their lives throughout the day, the Northumberlands and Ulsters prepared for what would prove a difficult fight along Route 11. Deployed on a ridgeline to the west side of the road, the Northumberlands had managed to hold on through the night and into the early morning of 24 April with help from the Hussars' tanks. But even in daylight, when the Northumberlands could call upon UN air strikes, Chinese reinforcements moved en masse across the slopes of Kamaksan into staging areas below the Northumberlands' ridge. The Northumberlands sniped at enemy positions, called in artillery fire and coordinated air strikes throughout the day, but it was clear that the Chinese were preparing to launch a major assault under cover of darkness.

The Ulsters, meanwhile, were dug in along the east side of Route 11. A and D Companies held Hill 398 – the northernmost point of the Ulsters' defences – while C Company defended a spur to the south-east of Hill 398, which protected A and D Companies' right flank. B Company remained about 5km (3 miles) to the rear, entrenched on the Hwangbang-ni saddle. This position overlooked the valley to the north and south, which meant that

3   As quoted in S.P. Mackenzie, *The Imjin and Kapyong Battles, Korea, 1951* (Bloomington: Indiana University Press, 2013), 85.

A Vickers medium machine gun and its crew. Despite its relatively low rate of fire, the Vickers was reliable and had a long range, able to provide much-needed automatic weapons fire at ranges of up to 4,115m (4,500 yards). (Popperfoto/Getty Images)

whoever held the saddle could control movement along Route 11. It was therefore a critical position to protect the Northumberlands' and Ulsters' route of withdrawal along the valley floor.

Led by Maj. Sir Christopher Nixon, the Ulsters' A Company bore the brunt of the action on Hill 398. Throughout the day, the Chinese 188th Division launched somewhere between 12 and 16 separate assaults on the hill. However, such brazen daylight attacks exposed the onrushing Chinese to well-placed artillery and air strikes. They suffered tremendous casualties. The Ulsters, meanwhile, used their anti-tank weapons to good effect against Chinese infantry. Ulster Riflemen discovered that their bazookas could have similar effects as grenades, but with a much longer range. At ranges of around 90m (100 yards), the Ulsters' bazookas proved devastatingly effective.

One of the strongest Chinese attacks occurred in the late afternoon, after white phosphorous smoke ignited the brush at the base of Hill 398. As the fire spread upwards towards the Ulsters' positions, some of the Ulsters had to abandon their slit trenches to avoid being burned alive, but Lt. Gordon Potts, commanding 1 Platoon, approached the situation differently. He ordered his men to crouch down in their slit trenches and let the fire continue to burn up the hill. Once the fire passed over the men's heads, Potts gave the order to face forward and open fire. Potts' men caught the Chinese in the open as they massed for their attack. Their concentrated rifle and machine-gun fire disrupted the attack and forced the Chinese behind cover.

Chinese assaults had stressed the entire I Corps line. Maj. Gen. Soule's 3rd Division had held its ground, but to the right flank, 25th Division was locked in a bitter struggle with the Chinese 15th and 60th Armies. To 3rd Division's left flank, ROK 1st Division had fought hard but was forced to withdraw several kilometres south of the Imjin River. Chinese casualties had been too high to exploit ROK 1st Division's withdrawal, but intelligence reports also indicated that the North Korean I Corps was preparing to join the attack. Seeking to protect 3rd Division's lines of communication to the rear, Soule ordered his divisional reserve, the 15th Infantry Regiment, to occupy blocking positions south of ROK 1st Division at Uijeongbu. In 29th

The Glosters' Drum Major Buss plays every bugle call except for 'retreat'. (Soldiers of Gloucestershire Museum)

Brigade's sector, Brodie deployed Lt. Col. Crahay's battered Belgian battalion to the key road junction of Routes 5Y and 11. By doing so, Brodie ensured that his supply lines remained open. It was an important decision considering the threat of Chinese infiltration into 29th Brigade's rear areas, and one that potentially prevented the entire brigade from meeting the same fate as the Glosters.

That night, the British infantrymen and their ROK and US counterparts who crouched in shallow slit trenches and stared down their rifle sights in anticipation of the next Chinese human wave attack could not have known that although they faced desperate odds, their staunch defence of a handful of hilltops had severely disrupted the timing and tempo of the Chinese offensive. The Chinese had five divisions – 60,000 men – crammed into a 16km-long (10-mile) area on the south bank of the Imjin in front of the ROK 1st Division and 29th Brigade. Because those two units had blunted the first waves of the offensive, Chinese follow-on forces were bottled up and vulnerable to UN air attacks, which caused significant casualties and further slowed the offensive's momentum. The Chinese were growing increasingly desperate for a breakthrough. Consequently, the night of 24–25 April brought what every British soldier expected: a series of strong Chinese assaults against each of the three British infantry battalions.

The first Chinese attacks targeted the Northumberlands' Z Company, which occupied the southernmost flank of the British positions on the west side of Route 11. Commanded by Maj. John Winn, Z Company had spent the daylight hours digging in and coordinating sectors of fire. The ridgeline was steep, rocky and over 180m (600ft) high, which made it difficult to dig slit trenches. Even so, the Fusiliers managed as best they could to prepare for the onslaught that they knew was coming. Having already suffered casualties while defending Hill 257 on 23 April, Z Company had been reinforced by an assortment of whichever headquarters and support troops could be made available. Major Winn recognized that his position was the key point of the battalion's defensive scheme. If the Chinese captured it, they could sweep up the ridge to the north and east into the valley below. The entire battalion could be surrounded if Z Company gave ground.

At 8.20pm, the first attack came. It was a probe to identify Z Company's lines. The main attacks began about an hour later with mortar and machine-gun support. The Northumberlands dealt with these assaults well until 1.00am, when Chinese troops seized a high point on the left flank. Lieutenant Sheppard, commanding 10 Platoon, counter-attacked and recaptured the position. Around 2.20am, the Chinese launched another, stronger push to take the ridge. As the fighting grew increasingly desperate, Maj. Winn and

Fusilier Ronald Crooks moved to whichever sector faced the greatest threat of a Chinese breakthrough. Crooks, armed with a Bren gun, fired down the slope at concentrations of Chinese troops while Winn tossed grenades. By the end of the night, Winn had thrown a total of 60 grenades. In some areas, Chinese soldiers broke into Z Company's positions. Hand-to-hand combat followed, with Fusiliers sometimes swinging shovels and wielding rifle butts as clubs. Z Company's wounded were piling up – by 3.45am, five men were dead and 25 per cent of the company had been wounded too badly to continue fighting. 'Walking wounded' were simply patched up and sent back to the fight. In these dire circumstances, Winn requested assistance from battalion headquarters.

After hearing Winn's report, Lt. Col. Kingsley Foster came up with a plan. The plan called for two attacking pincers: Y Company would assault along the valley floor to the base of Z Company's position while W Company was ordered to send a platoon to attack south along the crest of the ridge. It was almost dawn when the relief effort began. W Company's platoon gave the Z Company defenders an extra boost, but it was Y Company's attack that proved decisive. Y Company's move benefited from a thick mist that covered the valley floor. Unseen by the enemy, Y Company reached the base of the ridge below Z Company's rear and spotted a mass of Chinese infantry preparing to charge up the ridge. Y Company stormed straight into their midst with bayonets fixed, catching the Chinese completely by surprise and driving them back in disarray. At that point, with their last assault defeated and dawn breaking, the Chinese withdrew and regrouped.

The attack on Z Company was part of a larger Chinese attempt to break through the south-west sector of the British defences along Route 11. As one prong of the Chinese assault engaged Z Company, a second thrust struck the Royal Ulster Rifles' B Company, which held the vitally important Hwangbang-ni saddle 2.4km (1½ miles) south-east of the Northumberlands' Z Company. Chinese observation posts on the high ground of Kamaksan

A deserted slit trench formerly occupied by the Glosters.
(IWM, BF 10279)

'THE DEFENCE OF GLOSTER HILL' – A COMPANY, 1ST BATTALION, GLOUCESTERSHIRE REGIMENT ON HILL 235, APPROXIMATELY 6.00AM, 25 APRIL 1951 (PP. 68–69)

Low-lying, early morning mist was a common phenomenon during the spring in Korea. In the early morning hours of 25 April, a blanket of mist covered the valley floor below Hill 235 **(1)**, creating the sensation that the battle was being waged in the sky, among the clouds; a surreal aura described by many veterans of the Korean War. Although dawn usually brought a brief respite in the fighting as Chinese units regrouped from their night-time assaults, on this morning the Chinese continued to press the attack **(2)**. They were desperate to break through; knowing that the Glosters were surrounded, the Chinese sought to overrun Hill 235 and continue the offensive further to the south. The Glosters fought back with everything they had. Bren guns and grenades proved particularly useful at breaking up human wave charges **(3)**. Even so, Chinese troops approached within 20–50m (22–55 yards) of the Gloster defences, particularly in A Company's sector, as depicted here **(4)**. Chinese forces eventually overran Point 235 – the highest point of Hill 235 – but Gloster counter-attacks drove them off. Airstrikes and artillery fire eventually pushed the Chinese off the hill long enough for the Glosters to attempt their breakout.

called in mortar fire on B Company while infantry massed below the saddle. Next came long-range machine-gun fire from the south-eastern slopes of Kamaksan, which covered the infantry's advance. Despite suffering heavy casualties, B Company used grenades, small-arms fire and fire support from 170 Mortar Battery to fend off every Chinese attack. The line of communications connecting the Northumberlands and Ulsters to the rest of the brigade remained secure.

Crude wooden crosses on a Korean hillside mark the graves of two men of the 1st Battalion, Gloucestershire Regiment, killed in action against Chinese forces. (IWM, MH 31980)

As the Chinese attempted to surround the Northumberlands and Ulsters to the south, they also attacked the Ulsters' strongest position, Hill 398. At about 1.30am, the Ulsters' A and D Companies came under artillery and mortar fire, which was accompanied by illumination flares to reveal British positions in the darkness. Then came the bugle calls initiating the Chinese infantry assault. As the Ulster infantrymen returned fire with rifles and machine guns, 170 Mortar Battery and 45 Field Regiment delivered barrage after barrage on the attacking Chinese. The Chinese infantry moved in groups, rushing from one piece of cover – rocks, fallen trees or folds in the ground – to the next. When the Chinese got close enough, the Ulsters lobbed grenades, or simply rolled them downhill. One Ulster lieutenant later recalled that 'we killed many of them within twenty yards. I don't know how they got so close.'[4] As the Ulstermen poured fire onto the onrushing Chinese, Chinese artillerymen also found their mark. Nestled next to the hill on the valley floor, the Rifles' battalion headquarters came under enemy mortar fire, which forced the battalion staff to scramble for cover. Digging into the hillside, the headquarters personnel managed to survive with few casualties, but many tents and trucks were destroyed. Around 3.00am, a Chinese attack broke through D Company's position, but was followed by a swift counter-attack from the Ulsters. After two hours of tough hand-to-hand fighting, the Ulsters drove the Chinese back down the hill.

Hill 235

In the Glosters' sector, Lt. Col. Carne prepared for that night's onslaught by repositioning his forces. He drew his men into a tight perimeter along the most defensible areas of Hill 235. The hill's northern and southern faces offered the best approaches for an attacking force. Two spurs ran from the crest of the hill to the rice paddy fields below – one to the north-east and one to the north-west. On the southern face, the hill sloped towards the valley floor. Rock cliffs and steep, loose scree covered the western and eastern faces, making them less vulnerable to attack. Carne deployed Capt. Mike Harvey's D Company on the north-east side of the hill. Captain 'Jumbo' Wilson led the severely depleted A Company, which guarded the hill's north-west

4   As quoted in Andrew Salmon, *To the Last Round: The Epic British Stand on the Imjin River, Korea 1951* (Aurum Press: London, 2009), 194.

Captain Mike Harvey and several other Glosters who managed to break out from Hill 235. Harvey's unorthodox decision to head north-west proved successful. (Popperfoto/Getty Images)

spur. Support Company and C Troop, 170 Mortar Battery, now fighting as infantrymen, protected the battalion command post and the Regimental Aid Post. The combined remnants of B and C Companies, under Maj. Denis Harding, were responsible for defending the southern slope. The Glosters dug in as best they could. Where the ground was too rocky to dig proper slit trenches, Glosters piled rocks up into low defensive walls called 'sangars'. By this time, it was likely that the Glosters were surrounded by two Chinese infantry regiments and their supporting mortar and machine-gun troops.

The Chinese launched two major attacks during the night. The first began around 10.00pm and concentrated on the north-west and south-east approaches. In the north-west sector, Chinese infantry rushed forwards in no apparently logical order. Tactical formations had disappeared as the exhausted Chinese – many of whom had force-marched for weeks to reach their assault positions – staggered into the attack. Captain Wilson's A Company fired their rifles and Sten guns at the advancing human waves, but the deadly combination of Vickers medium machine guns, fragmentation grenades and artillery fire once again proved most effective. The Chinese, however, called in mortar fire of their own to cover the advance. When they could get close enough, Chinese infantry tossed grenades at the Glosters, purposely aiming higher up the slope so that the grenades would roll down into the Glosters' slit trenches before exploding. A similar situation occurred on the south-east slope, where Major Harding's mixed command of B and C Companies fought off a series of Chinese attacks before a second major assault on Hill 235 began after midnight. Like the first, this second attack consisted of human waves supported by mortar and machine-gun fire. A Company again bore the brunt of the assault, with D Company providing enfilade fire that struck the oncoming Chinese infantry as they scrambled up the north-west spur. The fighting grew so desperate here that the battalion's assistant adjutant, Capt. Donald Allman, left his administrative duties behind and gathered a hotchpotch of 17 men to assist A Company.

This photograph was taken after the battle, in May 1951, but it demonstrates how many vehicles fleeing Route 11 would have looked, with infantrymen clambering aboard in any available space. (Popperfoto/Getty Images)

The Glosters fought through the night until, shortly before dawn, the now-legendary 'battle of the bugles' occurred. As Chinese bugles blared in preparation for yet another assault, the Glosters' battalion adjutant, Capt. Anthony Farrar-Hockley, jokingly suggested that the British troops ought to respond with some bugling of their own. Carne liked the idea, and after scrounging up a bugle from another soldier, Drum Major Philip Buss sounded 'reveille'. Farrar-Hockley then famously ordered Buss to play every bugle call he knew with the exception of 'retreat'. At first, upon hearing bugle calls coming from the command post area, some Glosters thought that the Chinese must have broken through, but once they realized that this was a response to the Chinese bugle calls, a cheer erupted along the Gloster lines. When Drum Major Buss finished, all was silent for a moment. Dawn broke. The valley floor was covered in the early morning mist typical of the Imjin River valley, but the sun shone brightly on the hilltops above. It was a surreal scene, with the Glosters defending a position that seemed to be sitting among the heavens. Then came the most intense Chinese barrage of the battle. There would be no daylight reprieve for the Glosters.

DAY 4: WEDNESDAY, 25 APRIL

As the Glosters fought off waves of Chinese during the pre-dawn darkness of 25 April, senior commanders met to review the current situation. At 29th Brigade headquarters, a 4.00am meeting was scheduled to review the current situation and plan the next day's operations, but when Maj. Huth and the brigade chief engineer Maj. Tony Younger arrived, Brig. Brodie was fast asleep. Brodie had suffered the stress of commanding a brigade in battle for the past three days with little or no sleep. In an effort to finally get some much-needed rest, Brodie had taken sleeping pills during the night. It was not until 4.30am that Brodie was awake and ready to conduct the meeting.

THE RETREAT ON ROUTE 11

The withdrawal of the Royal Northumberland
Fusiliers and Royal Ulster Rifles along Route 11,
9.00am to 2.00pm, 25 April 1951

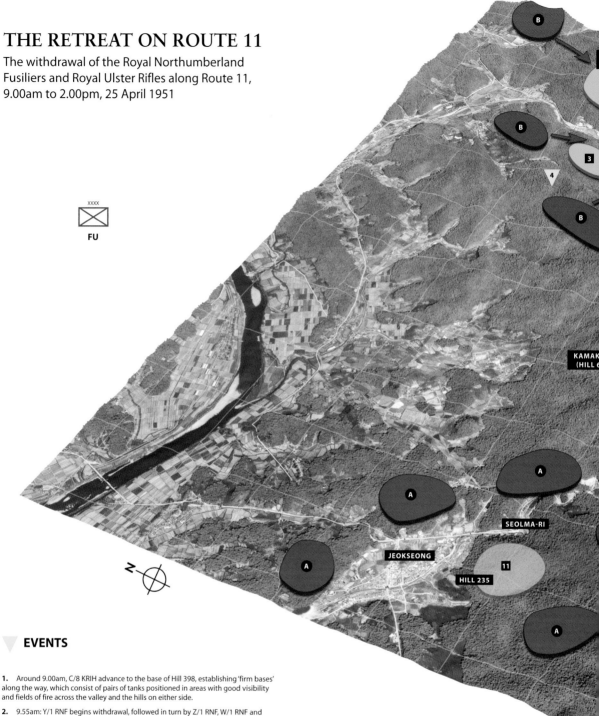

FU

KAMAK
(HILL 6

SEOLMA-RI

JEOKSEONG

HILL 235

▼ EVENTS

1. Around 9.00am, C/8 KRIH advance to the base of Hill 398, establishing 'firm bases'
along the way, which consist of pairs of tanks positioned in areas with good visibility
and fields of fire across the valley and the hills on either side.

2. 9.55am: Y/1 RNF begins withdrawal, followed in turn by Z/1 RNF, W/1 RNF and
X/1 RNF. The Fusiliers rendezvous with the advancing Hussars around 10.00am.

3. 12.00pm: 1 RUR, which was supposed to follow immediately behind 1 RNF, finally
begins to move, led by C/1 RUR, then A/1 RUR and D/1 RUR.

4. With the early morning mist dissipating, the Chinese can see that the British
have abandoned their positions. Chinese forces attack from the north and west in an
attempt to overrun the retreating British soldiers.

5. With the valley floor under heavy Chinese machine-gun and mortar fire, most
soldiers from 1 RUR take to the hills and withdraw across the more difficult, but better
protected, slopes east of Route 11.

6. Reinforced by a detachment of sappers from 55 Field Squadron, B/1 RUR holds
the Hwangbang-ni saddle against assaults from Chinese units advancing down the
slopes of Kamaksan.

7. Meanwhile, the Belgian Battalion defends the left flank of the retreating British
forces, protecting them from Chinese units that had captured Gloster Hill and were
now pressing on towards Route 11.

8. In the early afternoon, the Chinese ambush some of the last elements fleeing the
valley at an S-curve in the road. Hussar Capt. Peter Ormrod leads his tanks through
the rice paddies to the west of the S-curve in order to escape to safety.

9. Two Centurions commanded by Maj. Henry Huth provide supporting fire for
the retreating Fusiliers and Rifles. By 2.00pm, the last British units have escaped the
valley. Huth's tanks are the last to withdraw, following after the Belgians and the last
remaining battery of 45 FR.

74

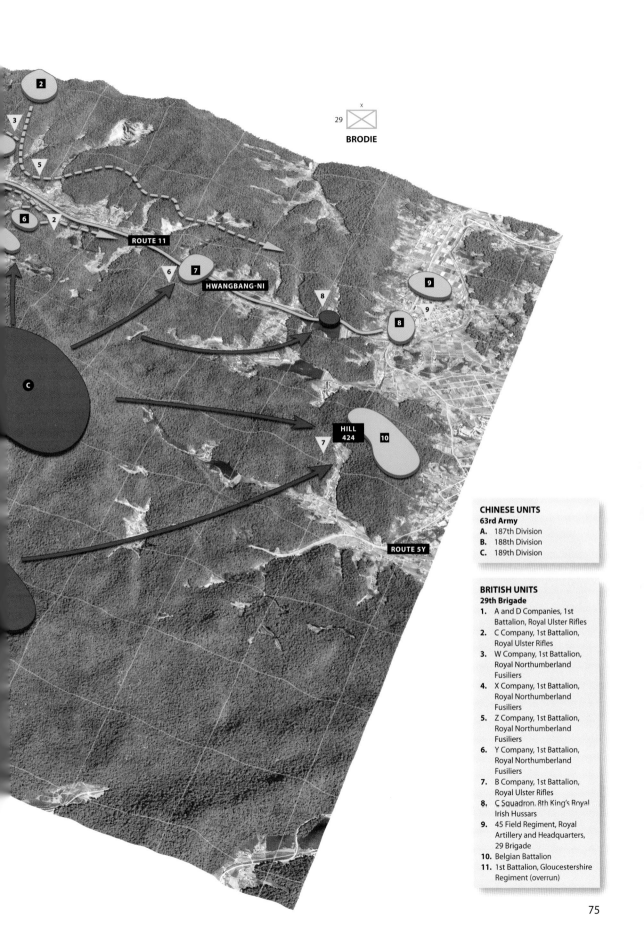

29 ⊠ X

BRODIE

ROUTE 11

HWANGBANG-NI

HILL
424

ROUTE 5Y

CHINESE UNITS
63rd Army
A. 187th Division
B. 188th Division
C. 189th Division

BRITISH UNITS
29th Brigade
1. A and D Companies, 1st
   Battalion, Royal Ulster Rifles
2. C Company, 1st Battalion,
   Royal Ulster Rifles
3. W Company, 1st Battalion,
   Royal Northumberland
   Fusiliers
4. X Company, 1st Battalion,
   Royal Northumberland
   Fusiliers
5. Z Company, 1st Battalion,
   Royal Northumberland
   Fusiliers
6. Y Company, 1st Battalion,
   Royal Northumberland
   Fusiliers
7. B Company, 1st Battalion,
   Royal Ulster Rifles
8. C Squadron, 8th King's Royal
   Irish Hussars
9. 45 Field Regiment, Royal
   Artillery and Headquarters,
   29 Brigade
10. Belgian Battalion
11. 1st Battalion, Gloucestershire
    Regiment (overrun)

How this lack of sleep over the past several days had affected his decision-making is a matter of conjecture, but the 30-minute delay had no effect on the Glosters' plight. The broader corps-level situation meant that no relief effort could be mounted.

When Lt. Gen. Milburn reviewed the situation at I Corps headquarters, he decided that the entire corps would have to withdraw to Line Delta. Soule's 3rd Division and Brodie's 29th Brigade were not the only units in trouble during the night of 24–25 April. To the right of 3rd Division, attacks by the Chinese 15th and 60th Armies had put the US 25th Infantry Division under severe strain. To the right of 25th Division, on the corps' far right, Chinese forces had infiltrated the US 24th Infantry Division's sector during the night, but were largely beaten back. The more pressing danger, however, was that the Chinese 60th Division had shattered ROK 6th Division's positions on the left of IX Corps. The Chinese had broken through the seam between I Corps and IX Corps and were now poised to strike US 24th Division's right flank and rear. On I Corps' left flank, ROK 1st Division had fought fiercely, but was pushed back 6km (4 miles). Furthermore, intelligence reports indicated that the North Korean I Corps had joined the attack, which meant that ROK 1st Division could expect to face additional pressure. Milburn worried that without falling back to consolidate his forces in new defensive positions, any one of his divisions could be cut off and destroyed in piecemeal fashion. At 5.00am, Milburn ordered I Corps to pull back to Line Delta, with the withdrawal scheduled to begin at 8.00am. Even so, he ordered Maj. Gen. Soule to do everything he could to rescue the Glosters before falling back.

Soule ordered Col. William Harris, commanding the US 65th Infantry Regiment, to go to the 29th Brigade headquarters and coordinate with Brodie to relieve the Glosters. But Soule had also been informed that Chinese units had infiltrated in force beyond 29th Brigade. Given the imminent withdrawal to Line Delta, he worried that the Chinese could attack to the south-east, seizing Route 33 and cutting 3rd Division's line of retreat to Uijeongbu. Soule had to protect Route 33, so he ordered two battalions of Col. Harris's 65th Infantry and the Philippine 10th BCT to secure it. He ordered Harris to deploy the 65th's remaining battalion along Route 11 to the south of 29th Brigade, which would secure 29th Brigade's line of retreat. As a result, the only units available to relieve the Glosters were a company of light tanks and a battalion of medium tanks. When Harris arrived at 29th Brigade headquarters, he conferred with Brodie and Huth. All agreed that the remaining units were insufficient for rescuing the Glosters. Brodie decided that the Glosters' only chance was to attempt to break out from encirclement on their own.

The Glosters' Last Stand

At 6.05am, Brodie radioed the Glosters' command post and gave them permission to break out. Up on Hill 235, Carne gathered his company commanders and issued orders. Due to the enemy's overwhelming numerical superiority, Carne knew that the Glosters could not break out as a single unit. They would be spotted easily and destroyed in the open. Instead, he gave the order for each soldier to make his own way back to UN lines. If soldiers moved individually or in small groups, they would stand a better chance of slipping away unseen. It was a difficult order to give, but it was not the most difficult of the day for Carne: he also gave the order for the wounded to be left behind. The Glosters had over 100 wounded men at the Regimental Aid Post who were in no shape to break out from behind enemy lines. These men would remain and become prisoners. The Glosters' medical officer, several medical orderlies and the battalion's chaplain, Padre Sam Davies, stayed behind with the wounded to continue providing care and comfort, despite knowing that they would surely become prisoners of war.

Riding atop the Hussars' tanks, British infantrymen were extremely vulnerable to enemy fire. (IWM, BF 10316)

As Carne prepared for the Gloster breakout, the fight on Hill 235 reached a tipping point. The Chinese had captured Point 235, the summit of the hill, which was located in A Company's sector. From this position, the Chinese could direct fire along the Glosters' entire position. The Glosters had to retake it. Realizing the danger, the battalion adjutant, Capt. Farrar-Hockley, gathered an ad hoc group together and launched a quick counter-attack. The counter-attack succeeded, but the small band of Glosters then had to endure seven additional enemy assaults. Farrar-Hockley's men only held on with the aid of 45 Field Regiment's 25-pounders. Throughout the early morning hours, the most intense Chinese assaults occurred in A Company's sector on Hill 235's north-west spur. D Company assisted as best as possible by directing enfilade fire into the flank of the Chinese attackers, but the situation remained desperate until the morning mist began to clear. With the increased visibility, American F-80 fighter-bombers swept in, dropping napalm on Chinese troop concentrations at the base of the hill. Those who were not killed or wounded by this gruesome weapon sought cover in ditches and shell craters. This took the pressure off A Company, which was badly in need of a temporary break in the fight – the company had fewer than 40 men who remained combat-effective. The Chinese continued to sweep the crest of Hill 235 with machine-gun and mortar fire, but the human wave assaults had stopped, at least for the moment.

The Glosters relied on heavy artillery fire and air strikes to suppress the Chinese at the base of Hill 235. Under fire, the Chinese would have greater difficulty intercepting the small parties of Glosters seeking to link up with the rest of 29 Brigade. By 10.00am, air and fire support had been arranged and the Glosters were prepared to move. Most of the men headed south, down Hill 235 and along the neighbouring ridges. Attempting a daylight exfiltration such as this was a risky prospect. From the heights of Kamaksan, the Chinese could easily spot any movement along the valley floor; Glosters who attempted to stay on the ridgelines would have run straight into the surrounding Chinese forces. With many men out of ammunition, the Glosters posed little threat to the Chinese. Chinese troops preferred simply to capture the survivors, often firing warning shots or yelling for the Glosters to surrender. Some few Glosters managed to hide in Korean homes or slip through the most difficult terrain, but the vast majority were captured. There were simply too many Chinese in the area.

The fate of D Company, however, was different. The company commander, Capt. Harvey, decided to keep his 81 remaining men together. He also decided to break out by taking the least predictable route – heading north-west into enemy lines, then looping further west before turning south again. Harvey intended to link up with elements of ROK 1st Division several kilometres to the Glosters' left. It was an inspired decision. D Company slipped down the north-west spur to the base of Hill 235, then turned west. At first, they only encountered a handful of Chinese. After about a mile, D Company turned south and followed a stream that ran below another high point, Hill 414. Here they were spotted by a US observation plane. The plane waggled its wings as a morale-boosting gesture to show the Glosters that they had been spotted. D Company was in luck, but they were also heading straight into a fight between elements of ROK 1st Division and the Chinese 192nd Division.

Colonel Kim Chum-kon, commanding the 12th Regiment of ROK 1st Division, had earlier that day ordered his 2nd battalion as well as two platoons of Sherman tanks from the US 73rd Tank Battalion to conduct a reconnaissance in force towards Hill 235 in an attempt to re-establish contact with 29th Brigade. The combined ROK-US force instead encountered a Chinese battalion that had been sent in a pincer movement around the Gloster defences. As the D Company survivors continued along the stream bed, they came under fire from Chinese forces in the surrounding hills. The men returned fire with what little ammunition they still had and rushed for cover. The Glosters continued to move south by bounding from one piece of cover to the next, but D Company was losing more men as the engagement went on. Around noon, American tanks from Col. Kim's reconnaissance force spotted D Company's men moving towards them, but from a distance the Americans thought that the Glosters were part of the Chinese force that they had been fighting. The Americans opened fire, wounding six Glosters. The observation plane, still circling above, immediately flew low to the ground and dropped a handwritten note to inform the tank crews that the oncoming soldiers were British. The tanks stopped firing, linked up with D Company and shepherded them out of Chinese small-arms range. By 12.30pm, the men of D Company were safe. Out of the 81 who fled Hill 235 with D Company, 46 made it out. A handful of others filtered back to UN lines over the next several days and weeks. In total, only 63 of the men who defended Hill 235 managed to escape. Over 500 were captured, including Lt. Col. Carne, Drum Major Buss and Capt. Farrar-Hockley. The Glosters had been destroyed.

Retreat on Route 11

Although Brodie was unable to prevent the loss of the Glosters, he was dedicated to extracting the rest of the brigade along Route 11. At around 6.00am, shortly before he informed Carne that the Glosters would have to break out on their own, Brodie informed his staff that the brigade had been ordered to withdraw to Line Delta with the rest of I Corps. He repositioned Lt. Col. Crahay's reconstituted Belgian battalion on a low ridge at the base of Hill 424 and adjacent to Route 11. This position lay about one mile south of where B Company, Royal Ulster Rifles occupied the saddle at Hwangbang-ni. The Belgians, reinforced by a troop of Centurion tanks, were ordered to hold on long enough to allow the Northumberlands and Ulsters to withdraw, but they were also responsible for protecting the brigade headquarters

The mortars of the Royal Ulster Rifles fire in support of the Route 11 breakout. (David Rowlands)

and 45 Field Regiment's artillery firing positions, which lay a mile to the east and within view of Chinese observers on Kamaksan. In essence, the Belgians held the western flank of the brigade's Route 11 defence. Brodie then placed the Northumberlands' commanding officer, Lt. Col. Foster, in charge of coordinating the withdrawal of both the Northumberlands and Ulsters from their positions overlooking the valley and Route 11 below. The Northumberlands and Ulsters would be supported by a mobile column comprised of Centurion tanks from Maj. Huth's Hussar squadron, sappers from Maj. Tony Younger's engineer squadron, as well as every Oxford carrier and half-track that could be found.

The mobile column would move first. They were to push 5km (3 miles) north from the brigade headquarters area, link up with the Royal Ulster Rifles' B Company on the saddle, then continue into the valley on both sides of Route 11 to protect the Fusiliers and Rifles as those units pulled back. The Hussars' lead troop commander, Capt. Peter Ormrod, conceived of a plan to establish what he called 'firm bases'. The idea was that as the mobile column advanced, tank sections would break off at intervals and occupy positions from which they could provide stationary fire support across the entire valley, thereby covering the remainder of the mobile column and the retreating dismounted infantrymen. Approximately 275m (300 yards) wide at its broadest point, the valley floor was filled with rice paddies, drainage ditches to irrigate the paddies, the occasional thatched-roof farmhouse and some scattered trees. Tank crews would have to establish their 'firm bases' in positions where they could cover large swathes of open ground while also being careful not to founder in the rice paddies or drainage ditches. The sappers would ride to the saddle, then dismount and reinforce the Ulsters' B Company. As the Northumberlands and Ulsters retreated south of each 'firm base' position, the Centurions would join at the rear of the column. Maj. Huth remained near the saddle with two tanks to coordinate between the Belgians, Hussars and the retreating infantry battalions. It was a good plan, but Chinese actions meant that it was to be executed far more chaotically than Ormrod had intended.

When the mobile column reached the saddle, Ormrod dropped off the sappers and left behind a troop of four Centurions as the first 'firm base'. The column then continued north, but two tanks slid off the road into rice

'HOSING OFF' – AMBUSH ON ROUTE 11, APPROXIMATELY 2.00PM, 25 APRIL 1951 (PP. 80–81)

During the retreat along Route 11, Capt. Peter Ormrod, led the Hussar rear-guard out of the valley. With the Rifles' B Company having already withdrawn from the Hwangbang-ni saddle, Ormrod's tanks crested the saddle at speed only to see that the Chinese had prepared an ambush at an S-curve further down the road. Ormrod did not want to risk driving his tanks straight into a prepared ambush, so he ordered his tanks to turn off the road **(1)** intending to bypass the Chinese anti-tank teams congregating near the ambush site. Armed with pole charges, grenades and Molotov cocktails, these anti-tank troops **(2)** could destroy a Centurion's tracks or light its engine on fire, but only from short range. The Centurions spread out among the paddy fields and rushed around the flank of the ambush, firing at the Chinese as they charged past. Unfortunately for Ormrod, the plan momentarily backfired as his tank drove head-on into a drainage ditch **(3)**. The driver switched the tank into reverse gear to back out of the ditch, but Chinese soldiers were closing in **(4)**. As they rushed towards the stricken Centurion, Ormrod pulled out his pistol and opened fire from the turret hatch, yet one grenade-wielding Chinese soldier had already managed to climb aboard **(5)**. Another tank commander radioed to tell Ormrod to close the hatch and take cover while he 'hosed off' Ormrod's tank **(6)**. Ormrod quickly shut the hatch as the other Centurion fired its Besa machine gun at Ormrod's tank. The machine-gun rounds riddled the side of Ormrod's tank with bullets, which did little damage to the heavily armoured Centurion but killed the enemy soldier and drove off the rest. Ormrod's driver eventually managed to reverse out of the ditch, and the tanks continued through the paddies. They were in the nick of time – the Chinese had by now occupied virtually the entire valley floor and were still streaming down the slopes of the hills to the west.

paddies. Disabled, the two Centurions could not move, but they continued firing at Chinese positions in the hills to the west of the valley. Small teams of Chinese infantry could be seen dodging between farmhouses and bounding across rice paddies. Many of these men carried pole charges and sticky bombs designed to blow the tracks off a tank or damage the engine to immobilize it. For the time being, at least, accurate fire from the Centurions' coaxial Besa machine guns kept these anti-tank teams at bay. By 10.00am, the Hussars had cleared the route and rendezvoused with the Northumberlands.

As the mobile column was advancing, Foster organized the Northumberlands' and Ulsters' withdrawal. He decided that speed was of the essence. The fastest way out, he surmised, was to head straight down the valley floor. The troops would be protected by artillery fire and airstrikes as they abandoned their hilltop defences. From there, dismounted infantry could move unimpeded while the tanks protected them. Some men, especially the wounded, could ride in or on top of the relatively fast-moving Oxford carriers and Centurions as they sped south along Route 11. With this in mind, Foster instructed Maj. Gerald Rickord, the Royal Ulster Rifles' acting commander, that when the order to withdraw was given, Rickord's men were to move with haste onto the valley floor. Rickord, however, thought the plan was idiotic. From the Ulsters' northernmost positions on Hill 398, Rickord's men would have to retreat over 8km (5 miles) to reach the relative safety of the brigade headquarters area. He believed that retreating through open ground during daylight would lead to a slaughter. Rickord asked brigade headquarters for permission to retreat along the ridgeline on the east side of the valley, which at least would offer his men some cover from enemy fire. The request was refused. He would have to move down the valley.

Across the valley floor from the Rifles, Fusiliers descended from the positions that they had defended for the past three days, scrambling down the steep slopes and into the valley below. Y Company led the way, followed by Z Company, the battalion headquarters, then W Company. X Company served as the rear-guard. They loaded the wounded into ambulances and half-tracks while those too exhausted to walk hopped aboard the battalion's remaining trucks and jeeps. Oxford carriers, jeeps and trucks filled the road in a haphazard convoy as Ormrod's tanks scanned the slopes for signs of Chinese movement. Men who remained dismounted moved tactically, spaced out at intervals to minimize the effects of enemy machine-gun fire.

The Fusiliers had begun their retreat, but by 10.45am the Rifles were still nowhere to be seen. Foster was upset. He knew that the Chinese would soon realize what was happening and renew their efforts to cut off the British retreat. The Rifles, however, had a longer distance to travel in order to reach their staging areas at the base of Hill 398, and had suffered from a friendly fire incident in which a stray artillery round killed several Riflemen from C Company. As the battalion filed into the valley, Lt. John Mole and his half-section of mortars fired round after round to cover the retreat. Once the battalion was underway, Mole's mortars followed behind.

It was not until 12.00pm that the Ulsters had recovered from the confusion and resumed their withdrawal. The low-lying mist had dissipated in the heat of day, which meant that UN aircraft could provide close air support, but it also allowed the Chinese an unobstructed view of the British retreat. From Kamaksan, the Chinese could see the motley collection of tanks, trucks, over-burdened ambulances, jeeps and dismounted infantrymen trundling down Route 11. Elements from the Chinese 188th Division had occupied the eastern slope of Kamaksan, while troops from the 189th Division had faced off against the Ulsters on Hill 398 during the night of 24–25 April. The Chinese quickly cobbled together a regiment-sized force to seize the vacated high ground and trap the British troops in the valley. Chinese soldiers flooded onto the ridgeline that had formerly belonged to the Northumberlands, and set up firing positions oriented towards Route 11. Chinese machine-gun and mortar fire soon rained down on the retreating Fusiliers. On the opposite side of the road, the Rifles came under fire, too. Lieutenant-Colonel Foster's plan was rapidly falling apart.

The Ulsters were exposed on the valley floor with little cover. Sensing the danger, Maj. Rickord ordered his Riflemen to do what he originally wanted to do – retreat along the ridge to the east of the valley. It became an 'every man for himself' retreat as the Ulsters rushed for the safety of the eastern ridgeline. Centurions fired their 20-pounder cannons at Chinese troop concentrations and the artillery continued to provide covering fire, but 45 Field Regiment could not sustain their usual rate of fire because they, too, had to withdraw. The brigade headquarters had begun preparations to fall back once the Northumberlands and Ulsters were safely extricated from their positions. These preparations included the artillery. One battery departed at 10.30am, another at 11.30am. The third battery remained behind to cover the rest of the retreat. As one Chinese force organized itself for an attack on the Ulsters, Lt. Mole's mortars once again came to the rescue. He ordered an emergency action, firing at minimum range to hold off the Chinese long enough for the Ulsters to rush from the open valley to the cover of the eastern ridgeline. The mortars broke up the Chinese attack before it could begin.

The Chinese concentrated against the saddle. If they could capture this position, they would cut off the retreating British battalions. The Rifles' B Company and the sappers from 55 Field Squadron held on, firing at groups of Chinese who had tried to creep in close to the saddle. Meanwhile, Centurion tanks provided suppressing fire to keep the Chinese pinned back. Ormrod's idea of establishing 'firm bases' with his tanks proved effective. Bolstered by the Centurions' 20-pounders and Besa machine guns, the patchwork force of Riflemen and sappers was holding, at least for the moment.

Lieutenant-Colonel Foster, who had arrived at the saddle while leading his Fusiliers off the high ground, coordinated the passage of lines as his troops surged through B Company's position. The convoy picked up speed as incoming fire increased. Oxford carriers, trucks and jeeps tore down Route 11 as quickly as possible. Small teams of Chinese soldiers sneaked through the paddy fields and drainage ditches. Armed with sticky bombs and pole charges, they tried to run alongside and toss their explosives onto British vehicles. In order to do this, the Chinese had to expose themselves to the withering firepower of the convoy. Riding in the back of open-topped trucks and Oxford carriers or on top of Centurions, Fusiliers fired Sten and Bren guns towards the enemy. Tank commanders stood up in their turret hatches and lobbed grenades at the Chinese. Since it was difficult to aim as the vehicles bounced down the track, accuracy was less important than maintaining a high rate of fire. The idea was simply to keep the Chinese far enough away from the convoy that they could not get close enough to throw sticky bombs or detonate pole charges. If a vehicle stalled or was too

damaged to continue, Centurion tanks would shove it off the road. The men inside would then abandon the vehicle and continue the retreat on foot or by clambering aboard the next truck or Oxford carrier coming down the path. By the time they reached the saddle, some Centurions had so many infantrymen sitting on them that tank crews were afraid to traverse their turrets because of the danger of knocking infantrymen onto the ground. Once most of his battalion had reached the saddle, Foster climbed into a jeep and drove further south with his men. Shortly thereafter, he was killed by a Chinese machine-gun burst.

By early afternoon, with the Fusiliers now south of the saddle and most of the Rifles moving along the ridge east of Route 11, B Company of the Rifles and the sappers defending the saddle had done their duty. They began to withdraw to the east, falling in behind the rest of the Royal Ulster Rifles. Most of the mounted column had escaped to the brigade headquarters area, but for those who were still en route, one more trial remained: nearly a battalion of attacking Chinese had established a roadblock about 3km (2 miles) to the south, at an S-curve in the road that made for an excellent ambush site. Several trees grew around the bends in the road, and drainage ditches sloped down from the roadside, which provided good cover and concealment for would-be ambushers. The steep bank ensured that vehicles heading down the path could not manoeuvre off the road and would have to slow down to navigate the curve. As the British mounted column approached, the Chinese laid a trap.

A British ambulance half-track was one of the first vehicles to fall into the trap. Trying to avoid the ambush, the half-track swerved and lost traction, slipping off the road and into a ditch. The medical officer on board and the wounded men he was evacuating found themselves surrounded by Chinese and surrendered. Using Molotov cocktails, sticky bombs and pole charges, Chinese infantry disabled a Centurion at the front of the S-curve. The next vehicle, an Oxford carrier, swerved around the tank but was knocked off the road by a tank that could not stop in time to avoid the collision. The Oxford slipped off the road and crashed into a ditch. The rest of the convoy tried to surge through, firing at Chinese troops who ran alongside the column, tossing grenades and firing at the speeding vehicles. One white phosphorous grenade landed on the engine deck of a Centurion, which quickly caught fire. The crew abandoned the vehicle but was soon captured. With British infantrymen packed tightly on top of the fleeing tanks, trucks and other vehicles, Chinese small-arms fire was having devastating effect. Some soldiers

Men of 29th Brigade take a break at the side of a road during their withdrawal to new defence positions. (IWM, MH 32809)

fell off the tanks after being shot, others were thrown off as vehicles lurched around the bend in the road. Aided by the Hussars' mobility and firepower, the Fusiliers and Rifles had reached the relative safety of the brigade rear area, but the fight was not over.

Having finished off the Glosters, by afternoon the Chinese had shifted forces from Hill 235 towards Route 11. Chinese troops were now attacking the Belgian battalion, which covered the western approaches to the brigade rear area, in strength. To the rear, Chinese mortar rounds were now impacting near brigade headquarters. To protect the headquarters, anti-aircraft guns of 11 (Sphinx) Light Anti-Aircraft Battery fired over open sights at nearby Chinese troop concentrations. Even so, Chinese infantry had infiltrated so close to the brigade headquarters area that bullets cracked in the air above Brig. Brodie's command post. Having held long enough to cover the Route 11 retreat, the Belgians pulled back under cover fire from two of Maj. Huth's Centurions. With the Fusiliers and Rifles now safely evacuated from their positions, Brodie could now order a general withdrawal. Around 2.00pm, with the rest of the brigade – minus the Glosters – heading south under covering fire from Huth's Centurions, the last battery from 45 Field Regiment limbered up and joined the column heading down Route 11 to the MSR (Route 33), about 5km (3 miles) away. The artillery had proved the difference in so many firefights during the battle; it was fitting that they would be among the last to leave the field.

Along the Imjin River front, the Chinese 63rd and 64th Armies had succeeded in breaking through the 29th Brigade sector, but had incurred heavy casualties. Estimates vary, but it is likely that the 63rd Army suffered approximately 7,000 casualties during the battle. The 64th Army suffered an estimated 10,000 casualties out of 28,000 men. Despite throwing 29th Brigade back and destroying the Gloster battalion, Marshall Peng's forces were too weak to push on to Uijeongbu. Fresh troops were needed, but they did not succeed in seizing Uijeongbu until 27 April. UN forces compiled their casualty lists on a monthly basis. For the entire month of April, UN troops lost 824 killed and over 1,800 missing. ROK troops suffered 518 killed and nearly 7,500 missing in action. During the Imjin battle, 29th Brigade alone suffered 1,091 casualties. Of those, 141 were killed. Over 500 Glosters were captured and had to endure two years of captivity in Chinese or North Korean prison camps. At a roll call one day after the battle, all that was left of the Glosters were 129 men – mostly men who were either on leave during the battle or in rear areas close to brigade headquarters when the battalion was cut off, although the survivors of D Company arrived a few days later. Two Glosters were awarded the Victoria Cross: Lt. Col. Carne, for his overall leadership, and Lt. Phil Curtis, for his actions on Hill 148.

Although the Glosters received much public adoration due to their last stand on Hill 235, the story of 29th Brigade at the Imjin River speaks to the comradeship and dedication of the British soldier more broadly. Like others who served during the battle, the Gloster adjutant Capt. Farrar-Hockley understood that the rest of the brigade was equally deserving of praise: 'Neither they nor the Glosters sought to be heroes; only to acquit themselves honourably and competently, one among another.' That, Farrar-Hockley concluded, 'is the best of the soldier's calling'.[5]

5 Farrar-Hockley, 136.

AFTERMATH

The battle of the Imjin River was over, but the Chinese offensive ground on. The assault across the Imjin was not the only threat facing I Corps. Although Brodie's men had delayed the Chinese advance long enough for the US 3rd Division to withdraw to Line Kansas and reorganize, Lt. Gen. Milburn's decision to withdraw to Line Delta was also influenced by developments outside I Corps' sector.

THE BATTLE OF KAP'YONG, 23–25 APRIL

On 22 April, to the east of I Corps, IX Corps' front was shattered when two Chinese armies from 9th Army Group attacked ROK 6th Division. ROK 6th Division was defeated in detail by similar night-time infiltration and human wave tactics as those used against 29th Brigade on the Imjin front. The Chinese 40th Army struck 6th Division's western flank while 20th Army broke through the ROK division's eastern flank. The Chinese objective was to penetrate as far south as Mudong-ni and Kap'yong, then wheel to the west and drive into I Corps, destroying the US 24th and 25th Divisions in the process. If all went according to plan, I Corps would be cut into pieces, with the Uijeongbu corridor assault slicing through 29th Brigade and US 3rd Division on the way to Seoul, as the 9th Army Group simultaneously encircled the US 24th and 25th Divisions.

The 6th Division retreat left a gap in the UN lines several kilometres long, which allowed the victorious Chinese to storm south along the Kap'yong River valley. On the morning of 23 April, IX Corps committed its reserve – 27th Brigade, another Commonwealth formation. From its assembly areas 35km (22 miles) behind the front lines, 27th Brigade was ordered to establish blocking positions on the heights above the river near the village of Kap'yong. 27th Brigade held a strong position on massive, steep hills along a front of only 6km (4 miles) – much narrower than 29th Brigade's front line on the Imjin. The narrow front allowed 27th Brigade to concentrate its forces, with 2nd Battalion, Princess Patricia's Canadian Light Infantry (2 PPCLI) occupying Hill 677 west of the Kap'yong River and 3rd Battalion, the Royal Australian Regiment (3 RAR) defending Hill 504 on the east bank of the river. In between the Canadians and Australians, 1st Battalion, the Middlesex Regiment (1 Middlesex) dug in on a ridge that dominated a large bend in the river. Supported by the 25-pounders of 16 Field Regiment, Royal New Zealand Artillery, the brigade was also reinforced by the M4A3E8 Sherman tanks of A

The battle of Kap'yong, 23–25 April

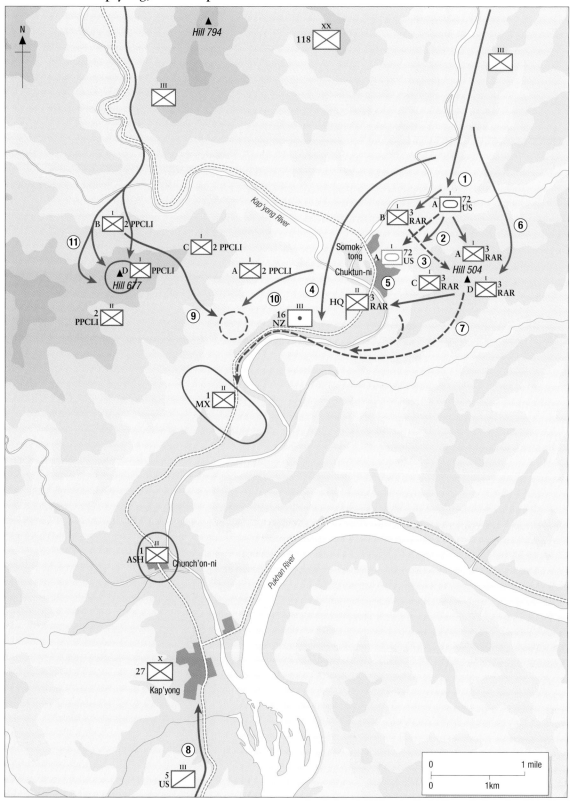

23 April:

1. 9.30pm: Fresh troops from the 354th Regiment of the Chinese 118th Division attack south toward a platoon-sized outpost of tanks from A/72nd Tank Battalion, on the right flank of B/3 RAR. The Sherman tanks disrupt the Chinese advance before falling back to their company headquarters. Despite withdrawing, the American tanks give B/3 RAR time to prepare for the onslaught to come.
2. The Chinese then attack B/3 RAR and A/3 RAR. Both units beat back numerous assaults throughout the night.

24 April:

3. After daybreak, and due to its exposed position at the base of Hill 504, B/3 RAR withdraws up the hill to join the main defence lines.
4. One Chinese battalion infiltrates between the 3 RAR and 2 PPCLI positions during the night. Once he discovers this, the 27th Brigade commander, Brig. Burke, withdraws 16 FR. The artillerymen re-establish a firing position in the brigade rear, near the headquarters. It was a prudent move, as Chinese infantry attacks the 3 RAR headquarters position beginning around 3:30am.
5. With their battalion headquarters under attack from Chuktun-ni to the north and the Chinese battalion to the west, D/3 RAR moves west across the slope of Hill 504 to assist. This relieves some pressure on the headquarters, but Chinese mortar and small arms fire begin to take their toll. 3 RAR headquarters retreats in good order to 1 MX lines, while D/3 RAR retreats eastward along a track through the hills before turning south to re-join friendly lines.
6. Around 10.00am, Chinese reinforcements arrive and begin assaulting 3 RAR on Hill 504. Airstrikes and artillery fire drive the Chinese away, but Brigadier Burke recognises the need to withdraw 3 RAR before they become isolated.

7. 5.30pm: 3 RAR begins a planned withdrawal from Hill 504. Despite Chinese efforts to pursue the retreating Australians, covering fire from A/72nd's Shermans and 16 FR's howitzers enables the remaining 3 RAR companies on Hill 504 to return to friendly lines with few losses.
8. During the night, reinforcements arrive in the form of US 5th Cavalry Regiment, which takes up positions near the village of Kap'yong.
9. In the afternoon, the 118th Division shifts its point of attack from Hill 504 to Hill 677 in an attempt to drive 2 PPCLI off of the heights. Sensing the danger, the 2 PPCLI commander repositions B/2 PPCLI from the north of Hill 677 to a spur on the battalion's eastern flank.
10. 10.15pm: Chinese troops attack B/2 PPCLI. Mortar and machine-gun fire breaks up several Chinese assaults.

25 April:

11. 1.00am: Chinese attack D/2 PPCLI, at the summit of Hill 677, in battalion strength. After intense hand-to-hand fighting and the company commander's decision to call artillery strikes onto his own position, D/2 PPCLI throws the Chinese back. It is a last-ditch attempt on the Chinese part, as they are exhausted from the fighting and have suffered heavy casualties. At dawn, Lt. Col. Stone realises that his battalion is cut off, with Chinese detachments blocking the roads and tracks linking 2 PPCLI with 1 MX below. Stone coordinates an airdrop for resupply and several helicopter evacuations of the wounded. Around 10.30am, the US 5th Cavalry Regiment launches a counterattack to re-occupy Hill 504, driving out the shattered remnants of the Chinese 118th Division.

Company, US 72nd Tank Battalion. Furthermore, in an emergency the brigade could call upon 1st Battalion, Argyll and Sutherland Highlanders, which had reached the end of its tour and was preparing to return home but was still present in the area. In the hills around Kap'yong, with the aid of airdrops to resupply the men with food, water and ammunition, the Commonwealth troops held against ferocious Chinese assaults until 25 April, when they were ordered to pull back 32km (20 miles) as part of Van Fleet's general withdrawal. By plugging the hole in the line left by ROK 6th Division, 27th Brigade ensured that the Chinese were unable to turn I Corps' eastern flank.

US Air Force C-119 Flying Boxcars drop much-needed supplies to men of 2 PPCLI during the battle of Kap'yong. (*Holding at Kapyong*, by Edward Zuber, Beaverbrook Collection of War Art, Canadian War Museum)

THE CHINESE OFFENSIVE STALLS

The battle at Kap'yong protected I Corps' flank, but even so, I Corps only held its new position at Line Delta for one day – 26 April – before withdrawing again. The next several withdrawals, however, were well coordinated so that UN forces would pull back short distances of 5–8km (3–5 miles) during daylight hours, where artillery fire and airstrikes could be called in on any Chinese forces attempting to pursue the retreating UN units. Artillery units also coordinated with each other, leapfrogging to the rear so that ample firepower remained stationary and on-call to support the infantry as other artillery units moved.

By 26 April, Lt. Gen. Van Fleet had begun to receive intelligence reports that indicated the Chinese offensive was losing momentum. 29th Brigade had seriously disrupted 63rd Army's attack, while 64th Army had also failed to strike ROK 1st Division as powerfully as intended. On 28 April, Van Fleet ordered I Corps to withdraw to Line Golden, 8km (5 miles) north of Seoul, and hold it at all costs. Engineers had been working round-the-clock since 23 April to turn Line Golden into a heavily fortified belt of trenches and strongpoints. Behind the front, dozens of artillery battalions were arrayed, ready to support the infantry and tanks. East of Seoul, UN forces began to dig in along what was called No Name Line. By 30 April, it was clear that a major Chinese assault on Line Golden and No Name Line was not going to happen. The Chinese had begun to pull back in order to consolidate their forces and reorganize. After seven days of nearly constant fighting, the first wave of Peng Dehuai's Spring Offensive petered out having failed to achieve its objective of encircling the bulk of US I Corps.

Forced marches and heavy casualties had exhausted the Chinese and caused them to overextend their forces. When UN troops withdrew more than a few miles, they could often rely on the use of trucks, jeeps and other forms of motor transport. The Chinese, however, had to march on foot, rapidly traversing steep ridgelines and jagged slopes as they chased after retreating UN forces. Furthermore, Chinese soldiers received little in the way of resupply during the offensive. After a week of constant fighting, Chinese units had begun to run low on ammunition, food and water. Heavy casualties also degraded the ability of Chinese units to operate effectively. Human wave tactics, by their nature, were expected to result in significant casualties, but this challenge was compounded by the fact that many company- and platoon-level leaders had been killed or wounded, which made the coordination of assaults more difficult.

Despite giving up ground and losing the Glosters, the overall UN defensive effort across the front was largely successful. Furthermore, ROK 1st Division and US 3rd Division protected the Munsan and Uijeongbu

Glosters at a roll-call held several days after the fighting. The bulk of the regiment was still missing in action at the time. (IWM, HU 61474)

Units of 29th Brigade stand at Parade Rest during ceremonies in which the American Presidential Unit Citation was awarded to the Gloucestershire Regiment and the 170 Independent Mortar Battery, Royal Artillery for their actions between 23 and 25 April 1951. (IWM, GOV 5300)

corridors. In addition, 29th Brigade's defence of the Imjin at the 'hinge' in which Line Utah met Line Kansas prevented a Chinese breakthrough in between ROK 1st Division and US 3rd Division, which would have permitted Chinese forces to encircle either division simply by turning east or west. With the exception of ROK 6th Division, UN withdrawals were largely deliberate, planned operations. The UN performance in blunting the 1951 Chinese Spring Offensive demonstrated how well UN commanders and soldiers had adapted to the circumstances of fighting in Korea against the Chinese.

On 16 May, Peng resumed the offensive with a series of attacks by four armies along the eastern half of the Korean Peninsula. The Chinese achieved some initial success by breaking through ROK III Corps along the Soyang River, but a series of coordinated UN withdrawals resulted in the Chinese overextending their forces. Low on ammunition and supplies, Chinese troops could not withstand the UN counter-attack that began on 20 May. Eighth Army pushed north to regain the ground lost during the April campaign. By 15 June, Eighth Army had reoccupied Line Kansas. From 22 April to 15 June, UN forces suffered over 39,000 casualties. Figures for the North Koreans and Chinese were far higher, estimated at between 90,000 and 105,000. The Spring Offensive marked the last time that Chinese and North Korean forces launched a major offensive designed to deliver a knock-out blow that would end the war. Instead, both sides settled into a war of attrition that raged as diplomats discussed the terms of a negotiated settlement – terms that would not be agreed for another two years.

Chinese troops look out from an entrance to one of many intricate tunnel systems dug during the second half of the war. (Sovfoto/UIG via Getty Images)

Eighth Army Advances, May–June 1951

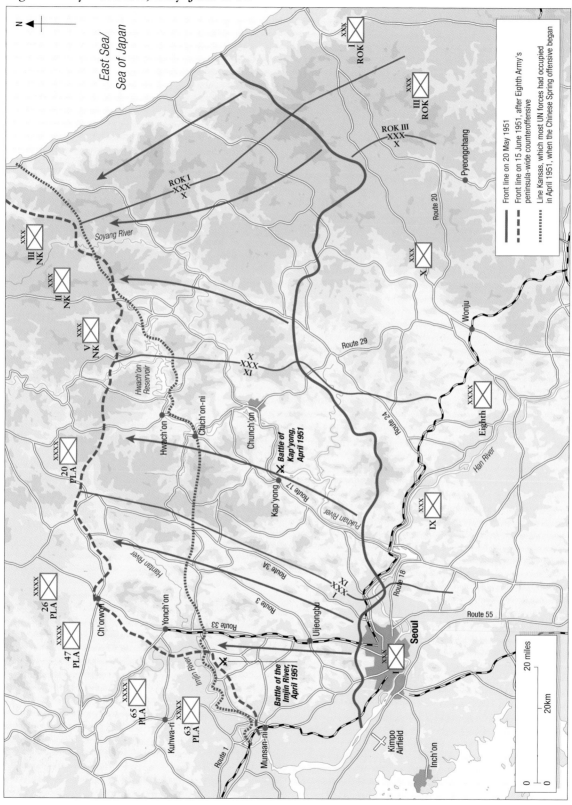

N

East Sea/
Sea of Japan

Legend:
— Front line on 20 May 1951
– – Front line on 15 June 1951, after Eighth Army's peninsula-wide counteroffensive
⋯⋯ Line Kansas, which most UN forces had occupied in April 1951, when the Chinese Spring offensive began

XXX I ROK

XXX III ROK

ROK III XXX X

Pyeongchang

Route 20

ROK I XXX X

Soyang River

XXX III NK

XXX II NK

XXX V NK

XXX X

Wonju

Hwach'on Reservoir

Chich'on-ni

Route 29

X XXX XI

Route 24

XXXX Eighth

Hwach'on

Chunch'on

Han River

XXXX 20 PLA

Kap'yong

Battle of Kap'yong, April 1951

Route 17

Pukhan River

XXX XI

Hantan River

Route 3A

XXXX 26 PLA

Ch'orwon

Yonch'on

Route 3

Uijeongbu

I XXX IX

Route 18

XXXX 47 PLA

Route 33

Route 55

XXX I

Seoul

XXXX 65 PLA

Kuhwa-ri

XXXX 63 PLA

Imjin River

Battle of the Imjin River, April 1951

Munsan-ni

Route 1

Kimpo Airfield

Inch'on

Scale:
20 miles
20km
0
0

THE BATTLEFIELD TODAY

South Korea has experienced rapid urbanization and economic growth since the end of the Korean War, which have transformed the landscape in major cities such as Seoul and Pusan. The Demilitarized Zone (DMZ), which is only about 10km (6 miles) from the Imjin River battlefield, still separates the two Koreas. The area around the battlefield remains sparsely populated. Towns and houses are sprinkled throughout the valleys and the road network has been greatly expanded since the 1950s, both in terms of number and quality. A bridge now spans the Imjin near the site of Gloster Crossing and a ROK Army base stands at the spot where Lt. Temple's patrol engaged the Chinese vanguard on 22 April. The ROK 25th Infantry Division is headquartered nearby; bunkers and trenches still dot the slopes of Gloster Hill, along with a small helipad. Many of these fortifications were built after the Korean War and remain in use today.

Several memorials lie at the base of the hill, where the Glosters' headquarters was initially deployed. The oldest of these is a stone memorial built into the hillside. Several life-size statues of Gloster soldiers, a large beret, a memorial wall and a small park now stand across a stream from the stone memorial. A commemoration ceremony is held every April. The park is often used for picnics and hikers frequent the area to enjoy a weekend away from the crowds of Seoul. Overall, it is a tranquil place.

BELOW LEFT
The older memorial to the Glosters, which sits in a shady glade at the base of Hill 235. (Author photo)

BELOW RIGHT
The new memorial and park opened in 2008 with a larger-than-life Gloster beret as its centrepiece, complete with back badge. (Author photo)

Fighting positions such as this one serve as a reminder of Hill 235's enduring tactical value. (Author photo)

On the eastern side of Kamaksan, several ROK Army units are headquartered on either side of what used to be called Route 11. The valley has more farmhouses, shops and vehicle traffic than it did in 1951, but the landscape looks much the same. The one exception is the presence of a reservoir on the west side of the road south of the Hwangbang-ni 'saddle'. This juxtaposition of heavily guarded military bases and mundane scenes of daily life reflect the reality of modern South Korea: a nation at peace, but prepared for war.

FURTHER READING

The Battle of the Imjin River and the 1951 Chinese Spring Offensive:
Li, Xiaobing, *China's Battle for Korea: The 1951 Spring Offensive*, Indiana University Press, Bloomington (2014)
Mackenzie, S.P., *The Imjin and Kapyong Battles, Korea, 1951*, Indiana University Press, Bloomington (2013)
Mossman, Billy C., *Ebb and Flow: November 1950–July 1951*, U.S. Army Center of Military History, Washington, DC (1990)
Salmon, Andrew, *To the Last Round: The Epic British Stand on the Imjin River, Korea 1951*, Aurum Press, London (2009)

Britain and the Commonwealth in Korea:
Farrar-Hockley, Sir Anthony, *The British Part in the Korean War*, Volumes I and II, HMSO, London (1995)
Grey, Jeffrey, *The Commonwealth Armies and the Korean War: An Alliance Study*, Manchester University Press, Manchester (1988)
Hennessey, Thomas, *Britain's Korean War: Cold War Diplomacy, Strategy and Security, 1950–53*, Manchester University Press, Manchester (2013)

General works:
Cumings, Bruce, *The Korean War: A History*, Modern Library, New York (2013)
Fehrenbach, T.R., *This Kind of War: A Study in Unpreparedness*, Macmillan, New York (1963)
Jager, Sheila Miyoshi, *Brothers at War: The Unending Conflict in Korea*, W.W. Norton and Company, New York (2014)
Millet, Allan R., *The War for Korea, 1950–1951: They Came from the North*, University Press of Kansas, Lawrence (2010)

INDEX